Succeed in
IELTS
Listening &
Vocabulary

ideal for both the
Academic
and the
General
Training modules

Andrew Betsis

Lisa Demiralp

Sean Haughton

GlobalELT
ENGLISH LANGUAGE TEACHING BOOKS

Introduction

IELTS is the International English Language Testing System. It tests all four language skills: listening, reading, writing and speaking. It is intended for people who want to study or work in an English-speaking country.

There are **two** versions of the test, the **Academic** and the **General Training** module. The **Academic Training** module is for those who want to study or train in an English-speaking university. University admission to undergraduate and postgraduate courses is based on the results of the Academic test.

The **General Training** module is mainly for those who are going to English-speaking countries to do secondary education or get a job and focuses on basic survival skills in social and workplace environments.

The **Listening test** is the **same** for both the **Academic** and the **General Training modules**, so this book is appropriate for candidates preparing for either of the two versions of the IELTS exam.

The **Listening section** of the test consists of **4 sections** with **40 items** in total and lasts approximately **30 minutes**. IELTS candidates will encounter many different task types such as: multiple choice, short-answer questions, sentence completion, notes, form, table, summary, flow-chart completion, labelling a diagram/map/plan, classification, matching.

Contents

Published by GLOBAL ELT LTD
www.globalelt.co.uk
Copyright © **GLOBAL ELT LTD, 2013**

Every effort has been made to trace the copyright holders and we apologise in advance for any unintentional omission.
We will be happy to insert the appropriate acknowledgements in any subsequent editions.

British Library Cataloguing-in-Publication Data
A catalogue record of this book is available from the British Library.

- Succeed in IELTS Listening & Vocabulary - Student's Book - ISBN: 9781904663911
- Succeed in IELTS Listening & Vocabulary - Teacher's Book - ISBN: 9781904663928
- Succeed in IELTS Listening & Vocabulary - Self-Study Edition - ISBN: 9781904663942
- Succeed in IELTS Listening & Vocabulary - Audio CDs - ISBN: 9781904663935

The authors and publishers wish to acknowledge the following use of material:
The photos in Units 1-10 © Ingram Publishing Image Library - © www.123rf.com Image Library

IELTS FORMAT

Academic Module	General Training Module
For entry to undergraduate or postgraduate studies or for professional reasons.	For entry to vocational or training programmes not at degree level, for admission to secondary school and for immigration purposes.

The test Modules are taken in the following order:

MODULE	QUESTIONS	TIME	QUESTION TYPES
Listening	4 sections, 40 items	*approximately* 30 minutes	multiple choice, short-answer questions, sentence completion, notes, form, table, summary, flow-chart completion, labelling a diagram/map/plan, classification, matching
Academic Reading	3 sections, 40 items	60 minutes	multiple choice, short-answer questions, sentence completion, notes, form, table, summary, flow-chart completion, labelling a diagram/map/plan, classification, matching, choosing suitable paragraph headings, identification of author's views, -yes, no, not given, -true, false, not given questions
General Training Reading	3 sections, 40 items	60 minutes	
Academic Writing	2 tasks	60 minutes	**Task 1** (150 Words - 20 minutes) Candidates have to look at a diagram, chart, or graph and present the information in their own words. **Task 2** (250 Words - 40 minutes) Candidates have to present a solution to a problem or present and justify an opinion.
General Training Writing	2 tasks	60 minutes	**Task 1** (150 Words - 20 minutes) Candidates have to respond to a problem with a letter asking for information. **Task 2** (250 Words - 40 minutes) Candidates have to present a solution to a problem or present and justify an opinion.
Speaking		11 to 14 minutes	It consists of three parts: **Part 1** - Introduction and interview **Part 2** - Long turn **Part 3** - Discussion
		Total Test Time 2 hours 44 minutes	

Lead-in questions

1. What sort of difficulties do people have when talking on the phone in a foreign language?
2. In which situations would you need to give your name and address to the person on the other end of the line?
3. If asked, would you be able to provide your address in your home country, or the one in England if you are staying there?
4. Practise spelling your name and street name to your partner.

(After completing the feedback on the lead-in questions, the teacher should encourage as many students as possible to spell out their names and addresses.)

Focus on letter recognition

This is unfortunately a largely neglected area as it is assumed that higher-level students have already mastered the alphabet. However, the ability to recite it does not mean that they are proficient at replicating what they hear on paper. Often non-native speakers mispronounce the sounds and therefore have difficulty recognising them from the recording. Apart from this, there are some sounds which may seem almost the same when listening under pressure. Remember that the recording is of an authentic-style dialogue and, most importantly, you will only hear it **once**.

Lead-in questions

Task 1 *(Here's a part of the audioscript for the Main Listening from this unit)*
Read the dialogue below and then answer the questions which follow.

A. Hello, this is Alistair Norseman. Is this the census helpline?
B. Yes, that's right. What can I do for you?
A. I wonder if you can help me. I got this census form through the post a few days ago and I'm not sure what to do.
B. Right. First, I'll need to take down some personal details. You said that your first name was Alistair.
A. Yes, that's right.
B. Is that spelt with a 'D' or a 'T'?
A. With a 'T'.
B. Oh thanks. I've got that down. And would you mind spelling your second name? Did you say it was Northman?
A. No, Norseman. And it's spelt N-O-R-S-E-M-A-N. You know, like the Vikings.

Comprehension questions

1. Why did the man make the phone call?
2. What confused the woman on the other end of the line?
3. Think about the sorts of problems a listener could experience when listening to this dialogue without the audioscript. Discuss them with a partner or as a class.

1. Because he does not know how to fill in the census form.
2. The spelling/pronunciation of the man's name.

3. Possible answers: the term "census" is probably unknown so this could lead to confusion over the context; the recognition of letters 'D' and 'T', and his surname; the spelling speed and the fact that it cannot be repeated.

(After completing the feedback on the lead-in questions, the teacher should encourage as many students as possible to spell out their names and addresses.)

Pre-listening practice

Now you shall do some practice exercises to help you recognise letters and improve your spelling speed.

Task 2 { Track 001 }
Listening for sound differences

Before the words are spelt out in the listening, you will hear the actual word itself. So it is important to listen carefully at this point to improve your chances of spelling it correctly.

The sentences below contain sounds which students often find hard to pick out. Put a tick next to the sentence that you hear. You will have to listen very carefully as the difference is very slight.

1. **a.** My name is Steve Newly.   _____
   b. My name is Steve Mewly.   ✔

   a. I live at 10, Thanes Close.   _____
   b. I live at 10, Staines Close.   ✔

2. **a.** That's Mrs. Melanie Ridgely.   _____
   b. That's Mrs. Melanie Bridgely.   ✔

   a. And the address is Charwood Crescent.   ✔
   b. And the address is Sharwood Crescent.   _____

3. **a.** You'll need to speak to Jane Price. _____
   b. You'll need to speak to Joan Price. ✔

   a. You can find us at the end of Beachcroft Road. ✔
   b. You can find us at the end of Beachcross Road. _____

4. **a.** It's Catherine – Catherine Millwell. ✔
   b. It's Catherine – Catherine Meilwell. _____

   a. My address is Ditchfield Way.   ✔
   b. My address is Tichfield Way.   _____

5. **a.** The name is Darren Knight.   _____
   b. The name is Daryl Knight.   ✔

   a. This is it - 102, Pine Court Place.   _____
   b. This is it - 102, Vine Court Place.   ✔

Task 3 { Track 002 }
You will hear three short dialogues and will be expected to spell names, addresses and post codes.
Remember that there will be a pause in the middle of the postcode and this means that you need to leave a space when writing it down.

Listen to these dialogues and write the spellings in the blanks.

3A
Write **no more than TWO words and/or a number** for each answer.

Name:	Martin **(1)** M-A-C A-D-D-A-M-S
Address:	263, **(2)** B-R-A-I-T-H-W-A-I-T-E Avenue, Newington, Edinburgh
Postcode:	**(3)** EH10 6PZ

3B { Track 003 }
Write **no more than TWO words and/or a number** for each answer.

Address:	Preston College
	(4) C-L-O-U-G-H-B-O-R-O-U-G-H Road, Preston
Postcode:	**(5)** C23 XAE
Head of the Admissions Department:	
	(6) P-R-I-S-C-I-L-L-A Winters

3C { Track 004 }
Write **no more than TWO words and/or a number** for each answer.

Address:	**(7)** W-H-Y-A-L-L-A Lodge
	(8) C-A-I-R-N-S Drive, Stepton, Brisbane.
Postcode:	**(9)** BRS 329

MAIN LISTENING

At the beginning of the unit a man telephoned a helpline to ask some questions about filling in a census form. This section will help you to consolidate the skills practised over the previous pages.

Task 4 { Track 005 }
Write **no more than TWO words and/or a number** for each answer.

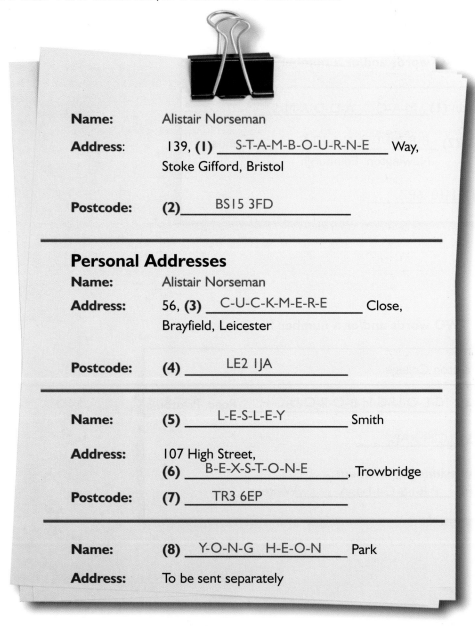

Name: Alistair Norseman

Address: 139, **(1)** ___S-T-A-M-B-O-U-R-N-E___ Way,
Stoke Gifford, Bristol

Postcode: **(2)** ___BS15 3FD___

Personal Addresses
Name: Alistair Norseman

Address: 56, **(3)** ___C-U-C-K-M-E-R-E___ Close,
Brayfield, Leicester

Postcode: **(4)** ___LE2 1JA___

Name: **(5)** ___L-E-S-L-E-Y___ Smith

Address: 107 High Street,
(6) ___B-E-X-S-T-O-N-E___, Trowbridge

Postcode: **(7)** ___TR3 6EP___

Name: **(8)** ___Y-O-N-G H-E-O-N___ Park

Address: To be sent separately

Post-listening Activity

Look at the different ways the word "**road**" is written in this unit. Make a list of them and try to find other ones. Becoming familiar with typically English names and cities from around the English-speaking world, particularly British and Australian ones, will also help you to feel more confident when listening for information in Part One.

(You may also like to write a list of typical British names –male/female first names, surnames and cities on the board. Or indeed elicit a list of stereotypically British names from the students – ask them to think of celebrities, pop stars and other famous people they know; ask them to name some of the famous landmarks and places in the English-speaking world etc.)

Using numbers

In this section you will hear the different ways of using numbers. Pay attention especially to numbers such as **ninety** which has the stress on the 1st syllable and **nineteen** whose stress falls on the 2nd syllable.
Remember that when the number is below 0, we use a **minus** symbol, e.g. **-2** (degrees).

You will also hear some long numbers during the IELTS Listening Test and must be able to write them down immediately. It is therefore important to become familiar with them. You can write them either as NUMBERS or as WORDS, but generally speaking it is advisable to use **numbers** as it is much quicker.

1. Lead-in questions { Track 006 }

Match the numbers **(1 – 5)** with the definitions **(A – E)**.

1.	68%		1 C		**A**	a ratio e.g. 5:2
2.	5.5		2 D		**B**	a temperature
3.	8:1		3 A		**C**	a percentage
4.	¾		4 E		**D**	a decimal number
5.	34 (degrees)		5 B		**E**	a fraction

Task 1

Listen to the examples in each category.

1. 13% - 84% - 60%   <u>51%</u>   <u>17%</u>   <u>48%</u>
2. 8.25 - 2.1   - 18.7   <u>40.6</u>   <u>15.33</u>   <u>20.8</u>
3. 9:6 - 10:1 - 20:3   <u>5:2</u>   <u>18:4</u>   <u>100:1</u>
4. 2/3 - 4/5 - 1/2   <u>1/4</u>   <u>9/10</u>   <u>7/8</u>
5. 24 (degrees) 41 (degrees)   - 10 (degrees)   <u>14(degrees)</u>   <u>-7 (degrees)</u>   <u>30 (degrees)</u>

Now listen again and try to write down the missing numbers.

Task 2

*(Here's a part of the audioscript for the **Main Listening** from this unit)*
Read the dialogue and then answer the questions which follow.

A: Hello Mr Preswick. Please take a seat. So you're interested in opening a student account with us.
B: Yes, that's right. You were recommended as the best option in the Student Union Gazette.

Focus on numbers in context

Questions

1. Who is speaking to the student and where are they?
2. What sort of advice do you think he will give and which type(s) of numbers from the previous exercise may be used?
3. If you were in the student's situation, what would your questions be?

Answers
1. Possibly a financial consultant or even the manager at a bank.
2. What type of account is the best for his purposes, overdraft facilities etc.
3. Answers may vary.

Task 3 { Track 007 }

Listen to how we say these long numbers.

1. 570   **2.** 908   **3.** 4,731   **4.** 1,430   **5.** 77,009

6. 18,091   **7.** 907,790   **8.** 665,925   **9.** 2,840,000   **10.** 68,036,876

Here are some more examples of long numbers. You should practise saying them first. Then listen carefully and underline the numbers you hear on the recording. { Track 008 }

1	a 512 b 520 **c 521**	7	**a 20,101** b 21,101 c 21,110	13	a 1,100,573 **b 1,010,573** c 1,001,573
2	a 115 b 116 **c 160**	8	a 64,234 **b 64,324** c 60,434	14	a 5,690,000 b 5,619,000 **c 5,609,000**
3	a 745 **b 743** c 735	9	a 19,409 b 90,490 **c 90,409**	15	a 7,542,104 **b 7,524,140** c 7,949,104
4	**a 8,950** b 8,590 c 9,850	10	a 305,350 b 350,305 **c 300,530**	16	**a 3,420,022** b 3,412,002 c 3,422,202
5	a 4,682 **b 4,692** c 4,629	11	**a 894,278** b 809,428 c 849,478	17	a 45,689,607 b 4,568,967 **c 40,568,607**
6	a 5,700 b 5,070 **c 5,770**	12	**a 570,367** b 517,367 c 570,357	18	a 12,000,500 b 12,050,503 c 11,050,503

Using Numbers

Remember that there are a **variety** of **longer numbers** which you may hear in the test, some of which will be read individually. One example of this is Telephone Numbers, e.g. 9-7-8-0-2-1-1. The last two numbers are the same and will therefore be: **double one**. This number also contains '0' which can be different depending on the context. In this case, you will hear 'oh' because it is in a phone number. Other examples are: **nought**, which is used with Percentages and Decimal Numbers; **zero** which is often used with long numbers such as the one on your Passport or that of your Driving Licence and also with Temperatures. Finally, though less commonly in IELTS, **nil** which is used for Team Sports, such as football, eg *The score is still 2-0 {two-nil}.*

MAIN LISTENING

Task 4 { Track 009 }

4A

In this section you will have to circle the letter of the answer that you hear and then fill in a table.
Look at questions 1 – 7.

1 How many students have an account with the bank? *(The proportion of students is in the darker shade.)*

a   **b**   **c**

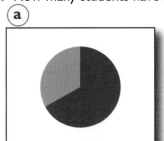   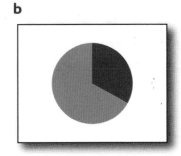   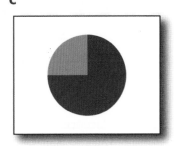

2 The maximum amount the student can borrow without paying interest is

          a   £250
          b   £215
          c   £520

3 There is a minimum yearly interest payment of

          a   5%
          b   0.9%
          c   0.5%

4 If the student borrows more than £1,000, the interest rises to

          a   5%
          b   1.6%
          c   0.6%

Saver Accounts	Annual Percentage	Duration
Short Term Saver	2.75%	**(5)** 1 year
Medium Term Saver	**(6)** 3.7%	2 years
Long Term Saver	**(7)** 4.15%	5 years

4B { Track 010 }

Now look at the following section and fill in the missing information as you listen.
Write no more than **TWO words and/or a number** for each answer.

Background Information

National Insurance Number:	**(8)**	PL 348600 H.
Driver's Licence:		NA
Passport Number:	**(9)**	943002939
Deposit:	**(10)**	£855
Other Account Number	**(11)**	56306672
Phone number:	**(12)**	258476

Post-listening Activity

Check how much you have learnt in this unit by completing this **True** or **False** section.
Write **True** next to the correct answers and **False** next to the incorrect ones.

	TRUE	FALSE
1	✔	
2		✔
3		✔
4	✔	
5	✔	
6		✔
7		✔
8	✔	

1. We say '**two to one**' when expressing the ratio **2:1** verbally.

2. It is a good idea to write down the number you hear in word form because this is faster.

3. The stress on **nineteen** falls on the first syllable.

4. The word **minus** is often used for temperatures.

5. National Insurance Numbers are read out individually.

6. You are very likely to hear the word **nought** in a telephone number.

7. **Two thirds** is the same as **75**%.

8. In a long number, the word '**and**' always comes before a number which is less than **one hundred**.

Unit 3 ON CAMPUS

Lead-in questions

1. Have you ever been to a university campus?

2. In general, what sorts of facilities did or would you expect to find on campus?

3. What sorts of problems might you encounter with these facilities?

Focus on predictive skills

Task 1

*(Here's a part of the audioscript for the **Main Listening** from this unit)*
Read this short extract from the audioscript and answer the questions which follow.
(The teacher will need to direct the students' attention back to the lead-in questions in order for them to fully utilise the first line of the listening dialogue.)

A: Excuse me. I wonder if you'd mind answering a few questions.
How much can you predict from the dialogue by looking at this first line?

(Think about who could be asking the questions, what sorts of questions they might be and why they are being asked. Also think about who the other person might be and how they will react. Will they agree to answer the questions or not? How do you know?)
(Possible answer: The language is formal therefore the questioner most probably does not know the other person. As it is on campus, we can assume at least one of them will be a student. Moreover, we can also ascertain that the speaker is going to note down the answers from which we can conclude that this will lead on to some kind of survey.)

Focus on the preliminary section

When listening, you will find that there is often an introductory part before it is necessary to answer any questions.
It is essential to elicit as much information as possible from this section in order to contextualise what you are listening to.
You can now read the continuation of the same dialogue in the next page.

Glossary

elicit *(verb)*– to take out the meaning from text
contextualise *(verb)* – to understand something more clearly from the situation it is in

Task 2

*(Here's another extract of the audioscript for the **Main Listening** from this unit)*
Read the dialogue below and then answer the questions which follow.

B: Will it take long? I haven't got much time. I've got a lecture in about ten minutes.
A: No, it won't take more than a few minutes and it will benefit you. You see, the Students' Union has put together this questionnaire to find out if there are any problems with the facilities on campus and hopefully come up with a few ideas with a view to solving them.
B: Oh, all right then if it's quick. I don't want to be late for my lecture.
A: Great. Right, first question; which facilities do you tend to use the most?
B: Well, I don't use the library as much as I should and I haven't set foot inside the gym.

Comprehension Questions

1. How does B feel? Is he willing to answer A's questions initially?
2. How does A persuade B to answer his questions?
3. Does B give a predictable answer to the first question? Why do you think he answers as he does?
4. Can you think of any reasons why he avoids using the library or gym?

Answers:

1. No, he is in a hurry.
2. She tells him it will be brief and that it is being done to improve on-campus facilities.
3. No he doesn't. We are expecting to hear which ones he uses the most first. Perhaps he answers as he does because he feels that he ought to use them more often and therefore feels rather guilty, especially in the case of the library.
4. Possible answers: lack of resources, understaffed, too crowded, etc.

GAP-FILL PRACTICE
Approaching **gap-fill** exercises in **Part One** and **Part Two** type questions.

You will have very little time to look at each section during the listening test so it is important to elicit the main idea from what you see on the page. This is done by looking at the title, if available, and underlining any key information in the text. Think about what kind of answer belongs in each space – e.g. a number, a place or a date. You should also consider whether it could be a noun, a verb or an adjective.
You may also find that there are some answers that have already been provided. You should pay attention to and underline these as they help you to follow the dialogue more easily. However, it is possible to miss them as they are not written in bold script and are often in a smaller font size.

Task 3 { Track 011 }

3A Write no more than **TWO** words and/or a number for each answer.

RESERVING A TABLE
Example: **Name**: Katherine Mackey
Group Size: 1 _____30_____
Number of tables: 2 _____3_____

Function Room
Hire cost: 3 ___Free/no cost___
- Decorate and select **4** __(own) music__

Deposit: Paid 5 days in advance **5 £** _10_ each

3B { Track 012 }

Write **no more than TWO words and/or a number** for each answer.

RESERVING A TABLE

* Cheaper on weekdays because of: **6** _special offer_

* Menu includes: meat and **7** _vegetarian_ options

* Tips included

* Website address: **8 www.oriental** _-garden.com_

* Date of the meal: **9** _(Thursday) 14th December_
* Time: 8pm
* Contact number: **10** _0786 587 644_

MAIN LISTENING

Task 4 { Track 013 }

At the beginning of the unit a student was being asked some questions from a questionnaire about campus facilities. We used prediction skills to analyse the first part of the dialogue and will now continue listening whilst completing a gap-fill exercise.

4A

Write **no more than TWO words and/or a number** for each answer.

On Campus

Example:
Facilities used: doesn't use the library or gym

Library:
* Good points: plenty of books
* Problems: difficulty understanding **1** _system_
* Solution: better database necessary with easier to understand **2** _instructions_

Gym:
* Good points: None given
* Problems: None given
* Additional info: outdoor pitches are in good condition
  Always someone to **3** _help / assist_ .

Cafeteria:
* Good points: cheap, nice food
* Problems: not much **4** _variety_
* Solution: rethink the menu
* Additional info: going into town centre: too time-consuming and **5** _expensive_. Cafeteria is clean, friendly staff

Parking:
* Good points: None given
* Problems: No **6** _parking space(s)_ after nine o'clock
* Additional info: 5-10 minutes to get to **7** _entrance_

4B { Track 014 }

Write **no more than TWO words and/or a number** for each answer.

Personal Information

* Academic year: **8** _____second / 2nd_____

* Member of the student union: **yes**

* Name: Michael **9** _____Braithwaite_____

* Age: **20**

* Current Course: **10** _Sports Journalism_____

* Address: **to be obtained from the bursar**

* Contact number: **11** _0774 562 008_____

Post listening activity

Look over the last three units and fill in the information below using the words **(A-F)** from the box. **NOT ALL** the words will be needed. Remember it is important to constantly use all the skills that you have learnt in order to make good progress.

A answers	**D** noun
B instructions	**E** introductory
C prediction	**F** reading

Evaluating the first three units

So far I have learnt that it is essential to pay attention to what is said in the **1** _introductory_ part of the listening. Another important skill is **2** _prediction_ which means trying to guess what is going to happen from the context. This is first done using the information from the **3** _instructions_ and then from the listening itself. Not only can you guess the type of word such as a number, name or time but also the word formation which is usually a(n) **4** _noun_ , verb or adjective. Finally, it is not only important to underline the words in bold but also to pay attention to the **5** _answers_ provided in the test even if they are less obvious.

Unit 4 — FINDING YOUR WAY ROUND

Focus on Map & Plan interpretation - 1

There are a variety of different locations which can be found in plan- and map-based listening activities.

First, you should read the instructions to understand the task clearly. There may be some differences in the language depending on the task and location. So, you must read the information carefully and think about how the diagram itself will be described.

You will most often hear one person talking but you may also hear a dialogue between two people.

Lead-in activity

Look at these extracts from five different dialogues and write the location where they probably take place next to them in the space provided.

Dialogues:

1. Over the wings, to your left and to your right, you will see an emergency exit on either side. _aeroplane_

2. Head straight down this corridor and go out through the door at the end. The Gym is the large building on the other side of the Playground, next to the Physical Education Hall. _school_

3. Well, if you take the first turning on your left and walk past the newsagent's and carry on for another 100 metres, you can't miss it. _street_

4. We'll be sitting in one of the middle rows in stand F. They're not the best seats in the grounds but we should still get a reasonably good view of the game. _stadium /football / rugby etc_

5. I reckon this is the best one for sunbathing, though there is another about 5km down the coast. _beach_

Task 1

1A Comprehension questions

Look at the map and answer questions 1-4 (this map is taken from the unit's **Main Listening**)

1) What do you think you will need to write on the map?
Letters representing the information because the spaces are not big enough for whole words.

2) Can you predict which place goes next to which number?
Answers may vary.

3) How much time do you think you might have to look at the map before the recording starts to play?
Answers may vary – approximately 20 seconds.

4) From which part of the map do you think the description could begin?
Answers may vary – the most logical is from the entrance and/or the lowest numbered answer.

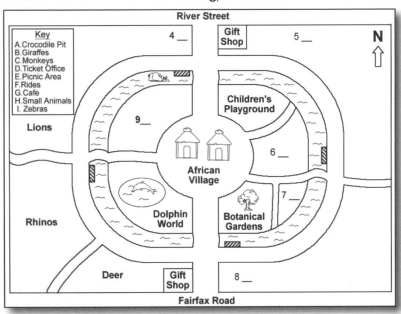

IB

Look at the extract below and then answer the questions (1-3) which follow.

Can I have your attention please? I want everyone to gather round and take out their maps. Right, open them up and find where we are now. Everybody should have found the gift shop near the River Street entrance. This is not to be confused with the one on Fairfax Road

1. Who do you think is talking to the students in the extract?

Tour guide

2. Where are they currently located?

The gift shop near the River Street entrance.

3. What mistake could a student make while listening to this extract?

They might think the gift shop was near the Fairfax Road entrance.

Focus on map and plan interpretation - 2

Approaching maps and diagrams in Part One and Part Two type exercises

It is important that you should think about the positioning of the labelled and unlabelled places both in relation to the starting point, which is often the entrance or may be marked on the diagram, and to each other before the task begins. While listening, you should pay close attention during the early part of the monologue/dialogue in order to understand exactly where you are on the diagram at the beginning. By doing so, you will be able to follow the rest of it more easily. You may have to write either words or letters on the diagram.

Task 2 { Track 015 }

Use the **numbers** in the diagram to write the answers in the spaces provided below.
Write **no more than THREE words and/or a number** for each answer.

I boat hire _____

2 children's playground _____

3 cafe _____

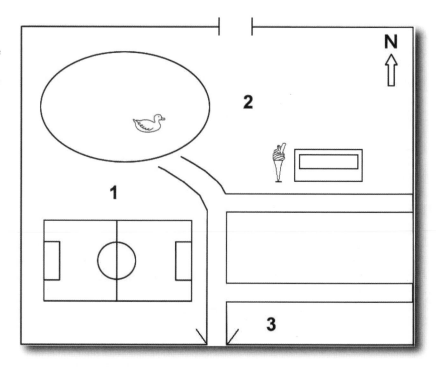

Task 3 { Track 016 }

Use the **numbers** in the diagram to write the answers in the spaces provided below.
Write **no more than THREE words and/or a number** for each answer.

4 TV lounge

5 kitchen

6 office

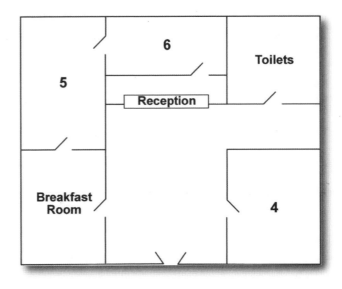

Task 4 { Track 017 }

Use the **numbers** in the diagram to write the answers in the spaces provided below.
Write **no more than THREE words and/or a number** for each answer.

7 6th-form College

8 grocer's (shop)

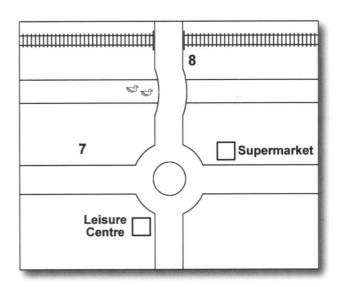

Focus on map and plan interpretation - 3

Plans and maps are often accompanied by other tasks such as multiple choice or open questions with two- or three-word answers. Remember, underlining key words such as nouns, verbs or adjectives in the question will help you to focus on the main ideas whilst listening. You will be given a short period of time between each task to allow you to study the next section before the recording resumes.

MAIN LISTENING

Task 5 { Track 018 }

You will hear a guide giving a group of students some information about a safari park and must answer the following questions.

5A

Write **no more than TWO words and/or a number** for each answer.

1. How long will the coach wait in the coach park?

30' / 30 minutes / half an hour

2. Which is the most enjoyable way of travelling around the Safari Park?

(by) boat

3. How frequently does the minibus service run?

every 15 minutes / every half hour

5B { Track 019 }

Listen to the recording and label the diagram using the letters **(A-I)**. Do not write the whole word in the space provided.

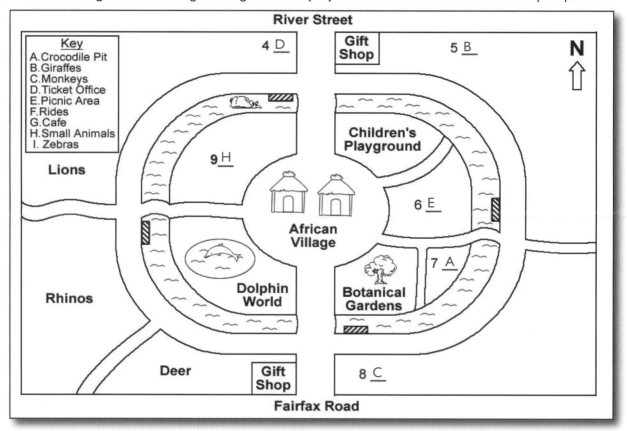

Post-listening Activity

In order to familiarise yourself with **Map Reading** there are a number of things you can do.

* Read the audioscript and follow the route on your map. Then listen and follow the same route again.

* Underline any parts of the dialogue that you think could confuse you and then decide why.

* Look at the diagram again and start from a different point. Think where other places are located in relation to that point, or think about which directions would be given if you changed the route. (*Try describing where each item on the map is in relation to a starting point of Fairfax Road. Then try the same exercise starting at African Village.*)

* Imagine you are describing your route from your house to another place, such as your school, to someone who does not know the area. Try to explain the journey.

Unit 5 OUT AND ABOUT

Lead-in activity

Here are five places where people go in their free time. Which one do you think is the most popular with young / middle-aged / elderly people?

cinema	art gallery	camp site
museum	theatre	

Below are **five lists** of **Nouns**. Each list is associated with one of the places above.
(1) Decide which list is associated with which place and write the place in the gap next to the list.
(2) Underline the one word in the list which is different from the rest – the **odd** one out.

1. impressionism, landscape, still life, stalls, abstract, portrait   ___art gallery___

2. stage, backdrop, play, performance, props, curator   ___theatre___

3. exhibition, soundtrack, display case, anthropology, artefact, sculpture   ___museum___

4. trailer, screenplay, subtitles, miniature, sequel, cast   ___cinema___

5. caravan, tent, sleeping bag, rucksack, gazebo, watercolour   ___campsite___

> ## Focus on Word Form recognition
>
> In the last four units, you have seen a number of gap-fill tasks, ranging from basic gap-fills and tables, to more complex maps and diagrams.
> The test requires that you should recognise different word forms, such as **nouns**, **adjectives** and **verbs**, in order to do these tasks well. Apart from this, you should also think about their position in the sentence.
> e.g. *an adjective often comes before a noun.*

Lead-in questions

Task 1

In the first part of the audioscript extract below there are some key words written in **bold**. You will need to put them in the correct category in the columns below. The first example has been done for you:
(key - RP = Radio Presenter)

RP: And here on **Radio** Southendean, we have a **special** guest, **Anne French**, the director of 'Never too far', the smash hit **musical** from the **West End** in London which **is** currently **touring** the country. And it's **being staged** for **three** nights, from the 22nd to the 24th of March at our very own Southendean Theatre. Welcome to our studio Anne. I'm so **glad** you **could make** it.

Verb	Adjective	Noun
(is) touring	special	Radio
being staged	three	musical
could make	glad	West End
		Anne French

IELTS Listening Unit 5

Focus on Gap-fill tasks

Verbs, nouns, adjectives and, in some cases, **adverbs** are known as **content words**. This means that they contain the most important information in the text. It is essential to remember that the number of words in each gap may vary - from one to three. This information is always shown in the instructions above the task and should be read carefully. In the 2- or 3-word answers you may find **prepositions, articles, auxiliary verbs** and other structure-related words accompanying a content word. However, these structural words are never used singularly and are not pronounced as clearly as the content words, so a good knowledge of grammar is important. There may sometimes be more than one alternative answer.

Task 2 { Track 020 }
2A

Write **no more than TWO words and/or a number** for each answer.

Cranfield Art Gallery

The art gallery is a piece of (1) ___modern___ 21st century architecture.

There are five acres of parkland around the Art Gallery which is
(2) ___two miles___ away from the centre of the city.

Its large windows allow in a great deal of natural light.

There are works by both local and (3) ___international___ artists on display.

(4) '___Lady in___ the Rain' was painted by a well-known Scottish artist.

You can find a variety of artistic styles including modernism
and (5) ___abstract art___ .

2B { Track 021 }

Complete the sentences below using **no more than THREE words** to fill each gap.

6. City Tours organises trips to the Cranfield Art Gallery every ___fortnight / two weeks___.

7. Students used to pay £3.80 until the ___end of January___.

8. The current student rate is not as high as ___(full) adult price / £6.20___.

9. You can either book your excursion online or from the reception of ___Students' Union Office___.

In this section, you will see that tables such as the one below do not always contain full sentences. However, it is important to remember that the same grammatical rules apply to all note-taking exercises.

Task 3 { Track 022 }

Write **no more than THREE words and/or a number** for each answer.

	The West of Scotland	The Lake District	Cornwall
Duration	a **(1)** _____ten-day_____ break	lasts for **(4)** _____fifteen days_____ and begins in late June	three weeks
Facilities	camping equipment is provided but you need to bring a **(2)** _____sleeping bag_____	(no information)	stay in **(6)** _____luxury caravan_____ meals catered for
Activities	hiking in the mountains, swimming and canoeing	orienteering, water skiing and **(5)** _____horse riding_____	water sports and outward-bound activities which include abseiling, **(7)** _____climbing_____, caving and potholing
Transport	You will have to **(3)** _____catch the train_____	the coach is included	(no information)

Remember

Remember that it is important to spell correctly when completing gap fill activities and that the words themselves in the first two sections, including the answers, will generally be frequently used ones.

MAIN LISTENING

Task 4 { Track 023 }

You will hear a radio programme in which a presenter is interviewing the director of a musical.

4A

Complete the sentences below using **no more than THREE words and/or a number** to fill each gap.

1. At the end of May, the director will be taking her musical on **(1)** (a) US tour/ trans-Atlantic tour .

2. Southendean Theatre is special for Anne because it was **(2)** her local theatre .

3. She began directing performances about **(3)** 12 / twelve years ago .

4. The first time she directed at Southendean Theatre, it **(4)** wasn't that/very good .

4B { Track 024 }

Write **no more than THREE words and/or a number** for each answer.

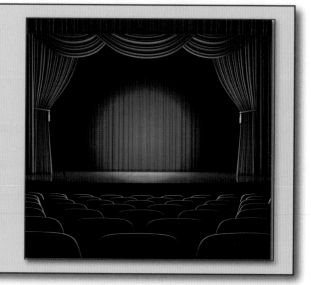

Laughing in the
Face of Adversity

- **genre:** drama

- first shown on stage **(5)** 3 / three years ago

- currently touring **(6)** Australian cities

Write **no more than TWO words and/or a number** for each answer.

Never too Far

- **genre:** musical

- about two children whose parents **(7)** _(have) died_

- after many years they are **(8)** _reunited_ .

- a good selection of music from **(9)** _(traditional) Irish_ folk music to American jazz.

4C { Track 025 }

Write **no more than TWO words and/or a number** for each answer.

Name of Play	A Place **(10)** _in Your Heart_
Genre	**(11)** _Romantic Comedy_
Plot	In the story, the two recluses are made to **(12)** _rely on_ each other.
First Performance	It's coming out in **(13)** _mid June_

Post-listening Activity

For each question, choose the correct form of the word (a, b or c) to fill in the gap. You may need to make small **changes** to the words, such as adding 'to' to a verb, or by making it **plural**.

1. Students can use their cards for _____ entrance fees.

   a. reduction
   b. reduce
   c. reduced

2. _____ should send in their forms well before the exam.

   a. application
   b. apply
   c. applicant

3. Remember to organise your groups of vocabulary _____.

   a. separate
   b. separately
   c. separator

4. What is the _____ between a verb and an adverb?

   a. difference
   b. different
   c. differentiate

5. It is difficult _____ which university to enter.

   a. decide
   b. decision
   c. decisive

6. A good vocabulary is _____ to succeed in IELTS tasks.

   a. necessity
   b. need
   c. necessary

7. There is a clear _____ between content and structural words.

   a. distinct
   b. distinctly
   c. distinction

8. Looking at the audioscript after listening is an _____ way of understanding your mistakes.

   a. effective
   b. effect
   c. affect

9. There are many ways of _____ your listening skills outside the classroom.

   a. development
   b. developing
   c. developer

10. You need regular self testing _____ you of your own progress.

   a. inform
   b. information
   c. informative

Unit 6 UNIVERSITY COURSES

Lead-in activity

Put the courses in the box below into their different university departments.

History, Psychology, Geography, Biochemistry, Computer Science, Medicine, Engineering Science, Archaeology, Economics, Law, Music, Chemistry, English Language / Literature, Art, Physics

Humanities	Mathematical and Physical Sciences	Medical Sciences	Social Sciences
History	Chemistry	Psychology	Geography
English Language / Literature	Engineering Science	Medicine	Archaeology
Music	Physics	Biochemistry	Law
Art	Computer Science		Economics

Focus on Part 3 tasks

You will have noticed in the first five units of this book that the dialogues are based on day-to-day situations which are typical of Part One and Part Two tasks. However, the second half of the book includes the more academic side of university life. These next two units will focus on tasks found in Part Three, such as conversations between two students or students and lecturers on topics more directly linked to their studies.

Task 1

In this extract from the Main Listening, two students are talking together on their first day at university. Read the extract and then answer the question which follows.

Gary Hi Judy. *(Judy: Hi)* I haven't seen you in ages.
Judy I know. It's been over two months now. I was wondering if I would see you here.
This was your first choice, wasn't it? (uhu) I'm so glad we got in to the same department.
Gary Yeah, me too. I was really nervous before they sent me confirmation of the course.
I spent three weeks checking my emails at least five times a day.
Judy Yeah, I know what you mean.

Focus on Prediction skills

How do you think the conversation continues? Write down four things you think they could talk about concerning their studies.

1. the number of hours per lesson
2. the amount / type of coursework
3. the way they do an assignment / homework
4. the lecturers / seminars

(Possible answers)

Focus on Distractors

You will hear in many IELTS listening tasks a number of distractors, which means that it seems that there is more than one possible answer to the question. It can sometimes be difficult to understand which answer is right and which one is wrong when listening, so it is important to listen to all of the information carefully in these parts. Underlining key words before listening and paying careful attention to the text during the listening activity will help you to predict the type of information you need to write down. It is also essential to consider the context of the possible answers before deciding on the correct one.

In the sections which follow, you are going to practise listening for answers in Multiple Choice tasks. You will need to choose the correct answer from the three possibilities.

Task 2 { Track 026 }

Choose the correct letter, A, B or C.

1. Which essay is Frances interested in talking about?

   a. the one on 'Educational Psychology'

   b. the one on 'Classroom Approaches'

   c. the one on 'The Future of Education in the Classroom'

2. What information is she not going to include

   in the first part of her essay?

   a. teacher training

   b. demographics and class sizes

   c. changes in testing systems

3. Which one of these ideas does she mention for the third part of her essay?

   a. How student behaviour has changed within the last twenty years.

   b. There are more single-parent families now than in the past

   c. interests and hobbies in the future

4. How does she feel about online learning at home for children?

   a. In the future, children will learn everything online.

   b. The only function of a school is to educate children.

   c. Internet learning at home is possible only if it is limited to a few days a week.

Task 3 { Track 027 }

Choose the correct letter, A, B or C.

1. Sarah felt nervous because

   a. too many people were watching her.

   b. she doesn't like Professor Stone.

   c. she realised the professor would be taking notes.

2. Sarah thought that Charlie's main weakness was

   a. his PowerPoint presentation.

   b. the accompanying music.

   c. the speech itself.

3. Charlie feels that he can improve if he

   a. spends more time on his visuals.

   b. provides more examples.

   c. reduces the length of his speech by two minutes.

4. Sarah is worried about her written work because

   a. her essays are too long.

   b. she feels her grades are low.

   c. she hasn't done enough essays.

As mentioned earlier in this unit, Parts Three and Four cover more academic subjects. For Part Three you will have to familiarise yourself with language which describes all areas of study, including course subjects, types of assignment, the university environment and so on.

Main Listening

Task 4 { Track 028 }

You will hear two new students talking about their courses and plans for the year ahead at university.

4A Write no more than **THREE words** for each answer.

1. How long did Gary have to wait for his email?   <u>3 weeks</u>

2. Where are they living at the moment?   <u>on campus</u>

Subject	Reason
3. Gary decided to study <u>Economics</u> .	**4.** He will be able to <u>earn big money</u> .
5. Judy chose <u>Archaeology</u> as her course.	She finds it fascinating.

4B Choose the correct letter, A, B or C. **{ Track 029 }**

6. Judy's booklist from the university contains
   a. 15 book titles.
   b. 55 book titles.
   c. 56 book titles.

7. Judy has to sign up for the trip to Egypt
   a. next month.
   b. in April.
   c. within ten days.

8. The Business Management project requires
   a. the use of pie charts and tables.
   b. each student to work with different groups.
   c. each student to do two presentations.

4C Write no more than **THREE words and/or a number** for each answer. { Track 030 }

9. They agree that the best way of taking notes is to use a <u>mini tape recorder</u> .

10. The students are required to provide their own materials; including books for their course and <u>stationery</u> .

11. Gary's first lecture is about 'The Influence of Globalisation on <u>World Trade</u> .'

12. The first lecture Judy has to attend starts at <u>10.30 am</u> .

Post-listening Activities

1. Here are two examples of questions with distractions in the answer. Underline the correct answer and put brackets around the distractions in the dialogue. Sometimes the answer will not contain the key word so you will need to understand the idea(s) behind the words.

a) Which city do you think is the best to study in and why?

"Well, I've studied in more than one place. The nightlife in (Manchester) was really exciting: concerts, theatres - there was always something going on. I spent a year in (Glasgow) and that was all right I suppose. The worst place was <u>Exeter.</u> There was absolutely nothing to do. <u>I spent all my time reading in the library</u>."

b) How much does the trip cost?

Rob: I don't know about you but I think it looks quite expensive. When we went last year, it only (cost £330) and that included everything. This time (it's £410) and it's for the same thing.

Gail: No, it's not. You're looking at the wrong one. That one includes an extra night in Paris and an excursion to Versailles. If you scroll down the page to Bargain Breaks, you can see that the trip you want only <u>costs £350</u> - not much difference from last year really."

2. Now, look at Task 4's dialogue; find the distractions and underline them. The first two examples have been done for you. Please note there will not be a distraction for every answer.

Gary   Hi Judy. (Judy: Hi Gary) How are you? I haven't seen you in ages.

Judy   I know. It's been over two months now. Did you have a good holiday then?

Gary   Great thanks. You?

Judy   Yes, thanks. I was wondering if I would see you here. This was your first choice, wasn't it? (uhu) It's nice to see a familiar face. I'm so glad we got in to the same department.

Gary   Yeah, me too. I was really nervous before they sent me confirmation of the course. I spent three weeks checking my emails at least **(five)** times a day.

Judy   Yeah, I know what you mean. So what did you think of the induction?

Gary   To be honest, it was a bit long. They went on for ages about each department and all the facilities. I didn't realise the university was so big.

Judy   Me neither. Are you staying on campus, then?

Gary   Yeah, for the time being. (Thinking of moving into a flat though, when I find my feet.)

Judy   Same here. So what are you studying? You were thinking of going in for Law last year, weren't you?

Gary   That's right. But my friends talked me out of it. It's far too competitive and it takes a long time to train. No, the future is in business. You know, trade and commerce and that sort of thing.

Judy   So, let me guess. You're doing the Economics course.

Gary   Yes, that's right.

Judy   But isn't that competitive, too?

Gary   Well, yes it is. But it's worth it. After I graduate, I'm in with a good chance of earning big money and I won't have to wait for years. How about you?

Judy   Well, I'm certainly not going into business like you – all those numbers and statistics. The one thing I can't stand is maths. Anyway, I've always been a bit of a History buff myself - and that's why I chose Archaeology. The course covers ancient civilisations from all over the world. I find it really fascinating. You know, we can learn so much about the present from the past.

Gary   Yeah, well you haven't convinced me. Digging around, looking for pottery and old bones – that's not my thing. Anyway, have you spoken to any of your lecturers, yet?

Judy   No, but I got emailed a whole list of stuff - about fifteen pages in all. The book list goes on and on. There are about 55 – no – 56 books we need for research and that doesn't include reference books.

Gary   Good job you've got the whole year to read them. You should have taken my course. I've only got a few books down on my list and half of them are optional. Most of the material is online. Did they send you any information on the coursework for the year?

Judy   Yes, but the last two essays were missing some information. Apparently, they are updating some of the assignments and we'll be told later on this term. It's not all essays, though. Next month, we've got to sign up for a big field trip to Egypt in April. We're there for a ten-day tour of the rock tombs and the pyramids along the Nile and we get to observe and assist in a dig. Then, when we get back, we have to write it all up in a report.

Gary   Lucky you. You get to go on holiday while you're studying. Our coursework isn't that exciting. We're doing an ongoing project on Business Management throughout the year – which includes designing a lot of questionnaires, graphs, bar charts – that sort of stuff. We have to work in the same groups throughout the year so everyone must pull their weight. And at the end of the year there is a big team PowerPoint presentation on the project and then individual presentations in which we assess our own performance within the group and any ways we could have improved it.

Judy   Well, you're going to be busy - and so am I. We've got a long list of essays to do starting the week after next, but that's okay I'm good at word processing. What concerns me is taking notes at the seminars and lectures. I hope that I can keep up. Only I'm not that quick at getting things down and when I try to write fast, I can't understand my own writing. Can we use an iPod or something?

Gary   Well, I don't think they're that clear when you are recording in a big area. Some students take photos of other people's notes afterwards but I think it's better to have one of those mini tape recorders – you know, the ones like the journalists have. I've heard they're really good.

Judy   Yeah, that sounds like exactly what I need, but where can I get hold of one of these recorders?

Gary   The university shop sells them. They're not too expensive either. How much were they? Umm … I think it was something like 20 or 25 pounds – Anyway, it wasn't too much.

Judy   Great. I haven't been to the shop yet so I can take a look around and buy whatever I need.

Gary   Well, you know that you have to supply your own stationery as well as text books. They've got a big selection if you need anything.

Judy   I don't think so. I've got all that I need - pens, pencils, notebooks – no difference from college, really. So what's your first lecture on?

Gary   Just a minute. It says somewhere on my handout. Here it is 'The Influence of Globalisation on World Trade' and that's first thing on Monday morning at nine o'clock.

Judy   Sounds like the perfect way to start your week (laughs). Rather you than me.

Gary   I'm sure it'll be okay. What about you?

Judy   Well, I'm luckier than you. Most of my lectures start after ten o'clock and I don't start mine until mid-morning on Tuesday and it says here that it's on 'The History of Archaeology', and it's from 10.30 to 12.

Gary   Well, good luck with that one. I think I prefer mine.

Judy   Anyway, I'm off to the shop now. Don't want to be late for lunch.

Gary   Okay. See you there then!

Unit 7 GETTING DOWN TO WORK

Lead-in activity

1. Two words sound like one when the previous word ends in a vowel (**a, e, i, o, u**)
   e.g. **speak about** sounds like one word '**speakabout**'.

   Read the following phrases aloud. Each one should sound like one word.
   a. write it up   **b.** a lot of essays   **c.** there's an idea   **d.** an important area   **e.** talk about it

2. Letters with a sound such as **p, b, t, f** and **k** are usually omitted if they are at the end of one word and the beginning of the next one.   e.g. **Jake Parsons** sounds like **Ja(-)e Parsons**. When the 'k' sound is omitted, the words become easier to say.

   Pronounce the following words:
   a. different people   a. differen(-) people
   b. speak fast   b. spea(-) fast
   c. student facilities   c. studen(-) facilities
   d. take photographs   d. ta(-)e photographs
   e. describe charts   e. descri(-)e charts

Focus on Joined-up speech

You will have noticed that it is often difficult to understand individual words when listening - even if they are known vocabulary. This is partly because of the **speed of speech** of the native English speaker, but it is also because they use linking and omitting sounds which aids fluency. It is important, therefore, to understand these particular rules of pronunciation in order to improve your listening.

Task 1

Here is an extract from this unit's Main Listening. However, the words are all joined together in each sentence. Separate them and highlight the key words only. Remember that it is **NOT** necessary to understand every word you hear.

Lecturer: Right. I'dlikeyoutotakeoutthehandoutsthatIgaveyouinthelastseminar. Ihopethatyou've allhadtimetolookatthem. You'llbereferringtothemalotoverthenextfewmonths.
The sentence has been started for you. Now complete the exercise.

Right. I'd like you to take out the handouts that I gave you in the last seminar. I hope that you've all had time

to look at them. You'll be referring to them a lot over the next few months.

Glossary
omitted: *not included*

Even though the questions in the listening are always answered in the same order as they are numbered in your test, sometimes you will find that the answer may be given before you hear the key word. This can cause confusion and therefore you should concentrate on the general meaning of each sentence as well as listening for the key words.

Task 2 { Track 031 }

Write **no more than THREE words and/or a number** for each answer.

Research Notes: Motivation in the Workplace

Maslow's Hierarchal Needs

Level One   **Physiological needs**
- water, **(1)** _____food_____, healthy body

Level Two   - **(2)** _Safety and security_
- housing, legal system

Level Three **Love and Belonging**
- humans need to bond and interact because they are **(3)** _____social beings_____.
- psychological disorders – lack of bonding

Level Four   **Self-respect and Respect from Others**
- employees with status and respect tend to be **(4)** _motivated and successful_

Level Five   **Self Actualisation**
- realising potential
- examples of achievements: setting up a business, studying for a degree, **(5)** _winning a medal_ in sports competitions.

Task 3 { Track 032 }

Write **ONE word only** for each answer.

1. The female student thinks that Maslow's theories are a bit ___old-fashioned___.
2. The two factors she mentions are categorised as ___hygiene___ and motivation.
3. Herzburg suggests that working long hours with very little in return can ___demotivate___ the employee.
4. He differs from Maslow in the way that he omits the more fundamental needs as he believes that since the beginning of the twenty-first century living standards have ___risen___.
5. He concludes that, in order to succeed, it is vital that we are able to work closely with others and that we should have a certain amount of ___control___ over our working environment.

Focus on Pronouns in word substitution

You will notice that in many cases pronouns such as '**it**', '**them**', '**that**', '**those**', '**this**' and '**they**' often substitute for NOUNS or NOUN PHRASES in order to avoid repetition. E.g. "Stress in the workplace has become more commonplace over the last few decades. _This is mainly due to the increase in the efficiency of communication through mediums such as the internet and the mobile phone._" The word '**This**' substitutes the noun phrase 'The commonness of stress in the workplace'.

Word substitution is a natural part of most languages and will most likely be familiar to you. However, when you are listening, it may be difficult to decide what the pronoun is referring to, and it (the pronoun) is generally unstressed so you may miss it while you are listening. In some cases, the word may even be completely omitted - if the meaning is obvious.

Main Listening

Task 4 { Track 033 }

You will hear a lecturer discussing how to approach the planning of a dissertation with a class of students.

4A Write **no more than THREE words** for each answer.

Dissertation Tutorial Notes

Basic information	Booklist	Learning Support	Draft Targets
• stages	• at least **(2)** _ten/10_ books	• tutorial about **(4)** _research methods_ advice	• compile bibliography
• necessary criteria	• first four **(3)** _books_ compulsory	• group discussion during the **(5)** _Thursday_ seminar	• to be submitted **(6)** _in November_
• page of **(1)** _helpful tips_	• brainstorm ideas		

4B Write **no more than TWO words** for each answer. { Track 034 }

Alternative Resources

Alternative Resources	• online materials have to be **(7)** _reliable_	• library archives	• interviews • **(8)** _tapescript_ must be included
Dissertation Targets	• hand-in-date, probably at end **(9)** _of April_	• length 18,000 - 20,000 words	
Specific Suggestions	• Look at similar **(10)** _dissertations_	• use computers in the **(11)** _Technology Department_	• contact the main office for **(12)** _insurance_ information

13. Which electronic equipment does he **NOT** mention?
Select **ONE** answer-option (a, b, c, d or e) only.

    a. mobile phone

    b. iPad

    c. tablet PC

    d. hi-fi equipment

    e. television

Post-listening Activity

Read through this unit again carefully and decide if the statements below are **TRUE** or **FALSE**.

1. If the first word ends in a vowel, the next word will be pronounced separately.

2. The sound of letters such as **p**, **k** and **t** are typically not heard when they come before a word beginning with another strong sound.

3. Understanding pronunciation does not help you improve your listening skills.

4. Sometimes we do not understand words in the listening even though they are known vocabulary.

5. When you are listening, the information for each answer always comes in numerical order.

6. The answer you are listening for always comes after the key word in the test.

7. Both understanding the overall meaning and the picking out of key words are important in listening.

8. Pronouns are used instead of nouns to make the meaning clearer.

9. You will only find word substitution in a few languages.

10. Nouns tend to be pronounced more clearly than pronouns.

	TRUE	FALSE
1		False
2	True	
3		False
4	True	
5	True	
6		False
7	True	
8		False
9		False
10	True	

Unit 8 MAKING HISTORY

Lead-in activity

Here are some academic words commonly used in IELTS listening tasks. Put the correct form of the word under each heading – in one case a single category will remain empty.

Noun	Adjective	Verb
preparation	preparatory	prepare
discussion	-	discuss
education	educational	educate
analysis	analytical	analyse
production	productive	produce

Focus on Part Four Tasks

In the next 3 units we will be looking at Part Four tasks. These are generally similar to those of Part 3 in the way that they contain academic language and take place solely in the university environment. However, the 4th part is usually a monologue given by a lecturer on a detailed academic subject - which you will often be unfamiliar with – in many cases, in the form of a lecture. Consequently, this part tends to be the most difficult, as it requires the most concentration and is at the end of the test.

Task 1

Read the extract from the unit's **Main Listening** and answer the questions which follow.

In this dialogue you will hear a lecturer addressing his students in a lecture hall.

Lecturer: Today we will be examining history in its most general terms and attempting to personalise it with questions such as **What does it mean to me?** and **How has it shaped the world that we live in?**.
Naturally, one lecture is hardly sufficient to cover such an extensive area but I hope to provide you with enough background information to inspire you to do more research for yourselves.

1. Do you think this lecture is at the beginning of or later in the course? How do you know? Because the lecturer uses the word introductory and uses the phrase 'general terms'. This is the case when the lecturer introduces a subject. It is only later on that he goes into more detail.

2. In what way does the lecturer try to make this lecture interesting? He personalises the lecture so that the listeners can relate to it individually.

3. How do you think he answers the questions that he mentions? Students' own answers may include references to techno-logical development, medical advances, political changes etc.

4. The word **examine** can be found in the dialogue. What is its noun? The noun is **examination**.

5. How about the verb for the word **information**? The verb is to **inform**.

6. Is the word **research** in the dialogue a verb or a noun? How do you know?
It is a **noun** because it is preceded by the verb {to do} and the adjective {more}.

<u>Glossary</u>: *monologue – a speech given by one person*

Focus on Word Form

When doing a gap-fill exercise, it is never necessary to change the word form. You will need to understand the structure of the question-sentence so that you are able to put the right word in the gap provided – exactly as you hear it (you cannot manipulate the word form to fit).

In summary, what you write in each gap must fulfil three conditions:
1. It must be (a) word(s) which is exactly what you heard on the recording.
2. It must fit within the allowable word limit in the instructions.
3. It must make grammatical sense in the context of the words surrounding the gap. (If it doesn't make grammatical sense, you should not manipulate the word form – you have simply chosen incorrectly. All you can do is have a guess if the chance to listen to the relevant segment of the recording has passed.)

Task 2 { Track 035 }

Complete the summary using **no more than THREE WORDS** for each answer.

Amongst the ancient indigenous peoples of South and Central America, two of the most advanced civilisations were the Olmecs, who were indigenous to the west of Mexico and the Chavin people found on 1 __(the) coast__ of northern Peru. Previously nomadic, they eventually built settlements and relied on 2 __farming and fishing__ for their livelihood. The discovery of archaeological artefacts has substantiated that they were not only literate but also engaged in 3 __religious worship__ The Aztec civilisation, however, was far more recent, lasting for approximately four hundred years until its ultimate collapse early in the 4 __16th century__. The Aztecs grew in power and 5 __wealth__, and at the peak of their powers they ruled over 10 million people. This was achieved by both the extensive trading of goods and the collection of 6 __taxes__ from conquered local tribes. There was also strong evidence to suggest that they followed a religion which included human sacrifice to their Sun god. Despite the bloodshed and cruelty, their society contained highly-skilled people such as musicians, 7 __engineers__, poets and sculptors.

Task 3 { Track 036 }

Write **no more than THREE words and/or a number** for each answer.

1. Thomas Savey's steam engine was used for _____pumping_____ water out of the mines.

2. Twice as much coal was _____produced_____ between 1750 and 1800.

3. The 'flying shuttle' was invented by _____John Kay_____ in the 1730s.

4. Richard Arkwright's spinning frame was powered by _____water_____.

5. The extensive network of canals made transportation of heavy goods _____faster_____ and more efficient.

Focus on Signposting

In Part Four listening, you will hear the lecturer use words or phrases which indicate the main stages in the lecture such as a **change of topic** or the **listing of key points**. These phrases are called signpost language as they help to guide you through the different parts of the lecture while you are looking at the test paper.

Here are some typical examples which you might find in a lecture.

Function in the lecture:	Examples:
Introduction	So let's begin with ...
Sequencing	Firstly ..., Secondly ...
Change in topic	Now, I'd like to turn to ...
Concluding	So, we've looked at ...

Main Listening

Task 4 { Track 037 }

You will hear a lecturer giving an introductory talk to students for their *Ancient History* course module.

4A   Write **no more than THREE words and/or a number** for each answer.

Introduction to History - Module One

Family Life

In North American and **1.** _____European_____ families, nuclear units are more common.
• *social affluence*

Young people have more freedom and **2.** <u>financial independence</u>
• *breakdown of the family unit*

But:

People living in countries that are **3.** <u>unstable economically</u> remain together for longer.
• *Britain - Second World War - stronger social cohesion*

Everybody works together – this term is called **4.** _____community spirit_____
• *Mumbai slums - substandard conditions - **5.** _____poor_____ sanitation.*

In many parts of the Middle East, **6.** _____religion_____ determines the social guidelines.

In this hierarchical system, the elders have great influence in the political system and in the social and **7.** _____family / familial_____ environments.

4B { Track 038 }

Write no more than **THREE words and/or a number** for each answer.

8. The earliest _____cities_____ were established in Mesopotamia by the Sumerians.

9. Herodotus, who was _____from Greece_____ by birth, is considered to have been the first historian.

10. Thousands of years ago, in primitive tribal communities, people fought _____for survival_____ .

11. Over thirty million people populate both the cities of Chongging _____and Tokyo_____ .

12. The population of Mexico City is predicted to have grown _____to 18.2 million_____ by 2015.

13. The trend in both Jakarta and Lagos indicates that the population of each city will _____increase_____ greatly over a short period of time.

14. Mass starvation could result from the growing number of people affected by the destruction _____of the environment_____ .

Post-listening Activity - 1

In this unit we have looked at signpost language and its role in guiding us through the monologues of Part Four listening.

In this section you should put the expressions into the correct categories in the columns below. In some cases the phrases may be put into two categories.

- Having looked at
- So we've seen that
- In the first part of today's lecture
- I will start by examining
- I'd now like to move on to

- First of all
- To sum up then
- Secondly, I'll explain
- Now, let's take a look at
- Finally, I intend to

INTRODUCTION	SEQUENCING	CHANGING TOPIC	CONCLUDING
In the first part of today's lecture	First of all	Now, let's take a look at	To sum up then
I will start by examining	Secondly, I'll explain	I'd now like to move on to	So we've seen that
First of all	Finally, I intend to	Having looked at	

Post-listening Activity - 2

Now, take a look at the audioscript for **Task 4** (page 80) and underline or highlight the same or other signpost words or phrases that you find, and decide which category they fit into. This will help you to understand how lectures are organised and you will therefore feel more confident when you are listening [refer to the audioscript in the Self-Study Guide].

Answers for the Tapescript Task 4:

1. Today we will be examining history in its most general terms (general introduction)
2. I'm first going to focus on the more personal aspect of what history means to us (specific introduction)
3. So far we've summed up some of the more evident reasons (summarising)
4. Now let's turn to (changing topic)
5. First of all, we need to take a journey (introduction/sequencing)
6. Now let's move on to the development of political systems (changing topic)

Lead-in activity

Finish each sentence (**1-3**) with the ending (**a** or **b**) which best describes the subject.

1. Biology is the study of
- (**a.**) the origin, form and behaviour of all living _species_.
- **b.** the relationship between the environment and our _ecosystem_.

2. Physics can be defined as
- **a.** the _analysis_ of how different forms of _energy_ are produced.
- (**b.**) the way _matter_ and energy _interact_ with each other.

3. In chemistry we learn about
- **a.** the chemicals which exist in all _organisms_.
- (**b.**) the _laws_ of how various chemicals change when they are combined.

Now put each **underlined** word from the exercise above next to its definition below.

___analysis___   a careful detailed study of something

___laws___   rules which are controlled by nature

___energy___   the force which causes things to move or work – e.g. electricity

___ecosystem___   the way all living things exist together – e.g. bacteria, plants and animals

___organisms___   individual animals or plants

___interact___   to have an effect on each other

___species___   different types or groupings of animals or plants

___matter___   the material all things are made of

Focus on comprehension in Multiple Choice tasks

It is important to remember that in the case of multiple choice questions, where you need to match the two parts of a sentence, not only should you underline the key words but, with longer questions, you should also try to quickly elicit the general meaning of the possible answers in relation to the question itself.

These (questions) will be in the order they are heard and will be testing you on different parts of the listening activity as it progresses.

In order to do this kind of task more effectively, you should concentrate on building up your vocabulary as you progress through the IELTS course. This will serve you well during the test as you listen out for paraphrasing of key ideas from the question (and answer options) as the recording plays.

Task 1

In this dialogue (taken from the Main Listening) you will hear a guest speaker talking to students in the Science Department. Read the extract carefully and answer the question which follows.

Good morning, everyone. I've been invited to talk to you about computer-controlled driving by your department. It may seem a bit of a cliché – cars that can drive themselves. You may also think that it could only happen in the movies but in truth it's more science and less fiction than it was – say - about twenty or thirty years ago. As you can tell from your ever-evolving phones and computers, technology never stands still. In fact, it has made tremendous progress over the last few decades and is continuing to do so.

Question

Which one of these options **(a, b, c, d** or **e)** is correct? Why are the other choices wrong?

The speaker states that computerised cars
     a. are already being driven by members of their department.
     b. only exist in the movies.
     c. have become a distinct reality over the last few decades.
     d. have been improved by using the technological know-how from phones and computers.
     e. are continuing to make significant advances.

Focus on complex Multiple Choice, Matching and Multiple Matching tasks

So far, in the previous units, we have looked at simple multiple choice tasks, where one of three possible answers has to be matched up with a statement. However, particularly in the latter sections of the test (which increases in difficulty from Part 1 to Part 4), the types of Multiple Choice tasks which appear may differ. There are 2 other types which are also commonly tested: Matching and Multiple Matching tasks. Examples of these types of tasks (taken from Part 2 of this book) are outlined below.

Multiple Matching

(answer options may be used **more than once**)

Questions 26-30
What does Elle says about the following subjects?
Write the correct letter, **A, B,** or **C** next to questions **26-30**.

> **A.** She will study it.
> **B.** She won't study it.
> **C.** She might study it.

Subjects

26. Marketing   _____
27. Human Resources   _____
28. Business Law   _____
29. Organisational Behaviour   _____
30. Finance   _____

Matching

(answer options may be used **once only**)

Section 2
Questions 11-13
Label the chart below. Write the correct letter, **A - E** next to questions **11-13**.

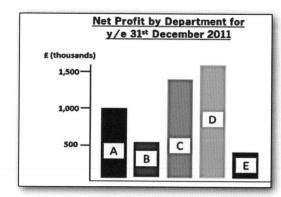

Net Profit by Department for y/e 31st December 2011

11. Online Sales Department   _____

12. Retail Sales Department   _____

13. Design Department   _____

Task 2 { Track 039 }

Questions 1-3

Choose the correct letter, A, B or C.

1. A tardigrade

     a. has eight legs.

       b. can only be found in seas or rivers.

       c. is made of approximately 1,000 cells which continue to multiply.

2. It differs from other invertebrates in the way that

       a. it darts around

     b. it has similar physiological characteristics to macrofauna

       c. its body is divided into eight segments

3. A characteristic of the tardigrade is

       a. it is able to walk.

       b. it has certain inner organs including a heart.

     c. it stores eggs for reproduction

Questions 4-6

Name **THREE** characteristics which make the tardigrade special:

       a. It is a deadly creature within its own environment.

     b. It can go into a dormant state if necessary.

       c. It has a lifespan of over 125 years.

     d. It can survive at temperatures of up to 303 degrees Fahrenheit.

       e. It is unnecessary for tardigrada to form a tun in freezing conditions.

     f. It disrupts the formation of ice-crystals by the production of protein.

Task 3 { Track 040 }

Write the correct letter, **A, B** or **C**. next to each statement.

> **A** horizontal-axis wind turbine (HAWT)
> **B** Dabiri's vertical wind turbine
> **C** qr5 vertical wind turbine

> **Hint:**
>
> Before examining the possible answers in each Multiple Choice task, pay careful attention to the instructions above. They will indicate how many points need to be circled while listening. This may range from one to three.

1. has got a 60-90 metre steel tower	A
2. is engineered in Britain	C
3. can be spaced anything up to a mile apart	A
4. derives its inspiration from marine life	B
5. produces the most energy for an individual turbine	A
6. quiet with little vibration	C
7. can be used in urban areas	C

IELTS Listening Unit 9

MAIN LISTENING

Task 4 { Track 041 }

You will hear a guest speaker talking to students in the *Science Department* of a university.

4A

Questions 1 - 3

Choose the correct letter, A, B or C.

1. The speaker says that owning a car
   a. can be stressful.
   b. incurs high running costs.
   c. is seen as a necessity.

2. During the earlier history of autonomous vehicles
   a. the first one was operated by a robot.
   b. the European commission started up a fund in the 1980s.
   c. the American army vehicles were built solely for off-road purposes.

3. A preliminary requirement of an autonomous car is
   a. the installation of additional road infrastructure.
   b. stringent testing of both hardware and software.
   c. a navigational system which includes sensor noise.

4B { Track 042 }

Questions 4 - 6

Which **3 benefits** of autonomous cars does he mention?

a. They are easier to park.
b. They are programmed for unexpected situations.
c. It is far safer than if a person drives.
d. There is no need for health and safety checks.
e. There are no fluctuations in their performance.
f. They feature a driver assistive system.

Questions 7 – 9

What are the **3 problems** mentioned?

a. Most deaths of young people are caused on the roads.
b. There were 2,222 injuries on the roads.
c. Fewer people were injured on British roads in 2010 than in previous years.
d. The impact of casualties on the National Health System.
e. The rise of car insurance premiums.
f. The occurrence of mechanical failure.

Post-listening activity

Complete the summary on the characteristics of **Multiple Choice questions** by using the words from the box below. There are **two words** that you will **not need** to use. Each word can only be used **ONCE**.

grammatical	underline	instructions	distractors
forget	letters	main	easier
clue	drop	vary	

Multiple choice questions may seem to be an **1** _easier_ option than some of the others. However, this is not always the case. Firstly, you will find that there are no **2** _grammatical_ errors which could provide you with a **3** _clue_ to the correct answer; and, secondly, before you listen, you will notice that all the answers seem to be, to some extent, logical. Another thing that you need to be aware of is that the number of answers given may **4** _vary_ from one to three, so you should always read the **5** _instructions_ carefully before listening. Each of the correct answers you **6** _forget_ to circle means you will **7** _drop_ a point. You should always remember also that the incorrect answers are usually **8** _distractors_, so you should look at the ideas - not just the key words - although it is still important to **9** _underline_ these.

Lead-in activity

Read the paragraph carefully and choose the most suitable answers from the charts below.

GLOBAL SPACE CENTRE

The complex itself was set up as an aerodrome back in the late 1960s. After having been in operation for just over twenty years, it was bought by the space commission, extensively renovated, and, in 1994, reopened as the Global Space Centre. The centre itself entertains a stream of visitors every year and their number has grown steadily since its opening. To illustrate this, back in 1994 the figure stood at approximately 2,500. By 2010, it had risen to a respectable 12,100 per annum, and this pattern of increase is expected to continue for the next decade. The centre houses both interactive and informative displays, catering for old and young alike. It's not all fun and games though; we at Global take the educational side of things very seriously as well. This year alone we've held 360 talks and seminars on over 80 different space-related subjects. Most, but by no means all of these, are put on for schools and colleges, which account for around 45% of activity in this regard; followed by universities at 38%; and the remainder are arranged by privately-organised groups and tours.

Statistics for the Global Space Centre

1. Number of Visitors

For the bar charts labelled 'Number of Visitors' the answer is **A** because of the phrase 'has grown steadily.'

A.

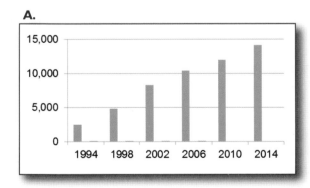

B.

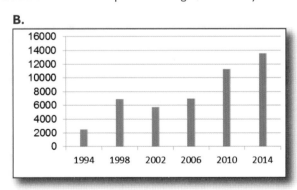

2. Talks and Seminars

For the pie charts labelled 'Talks and Seminars' the answer is **B** because the proportion of university students attending is too low in the other one.

A.

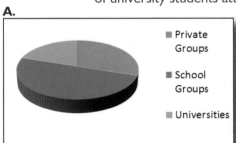

B.

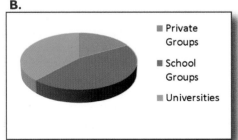

Focus on Charts and Diagrams

In the Part Four task you may come across charts and diagrams. The charts usually take the form of a bar or pie chart as shown in the examples in the lead-in section. There are other types of diagrams that you will have to familiarise yourself with, too, such as the flow chart, which may show progression or a cycle, and picture diagrams, which may illustrate a variety of things - the labelling of a piece of equipment, a natural process or how something works etc.

Task 1

In this extract (taken from the unit's Main Listening), the speaker addresses students at the *Global Space Centre*. Read through the extract carefully.

Hello, I'm Barbara Wilson and my talk is on inhabitable worlds. It may seem strange but, ever since I was child, I have looked up at the skies and wondered whether there are other people on other planets doing exactly the same thing as me. Perhaps we are a mere pinpoint of light amongst millions of others in the skies. The question is; where do we start looking? The time-honoured expression 'a needle in a haystack' comes to mind, but there are certain criteria which may help us to narrow down the odds.

Here is a diagram that could come up in the course of the speech. Using a **maximum of three words**, try to guess what could be written next to each number.

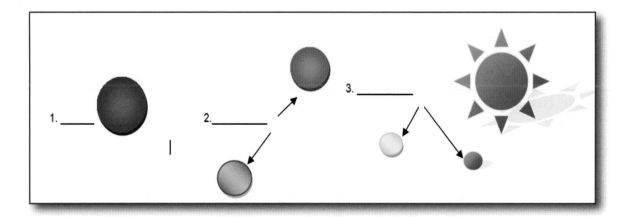

Possible answers for the diagram
1. too cold / too far (from sun)
2. habitable (worlds) / could support life
3. too hot / too near (the sun)

Focus on language

You will notice that the language will vary according to the diagram or chart. For example, a flow chart will often include the passive when describing a process but may also use active verbs in the case of a natural cycle. Therefore, it is important to pay attention to both the tense and the sentence structure in the chart before listening.

Task 2 { Track 043 }

2A   Questions 1 - 4

Write **no more than FOUR words or a number** for each answer.

[**Note**: in the actual exam you will never be asked to write **more than THREE words and/or a number**.]

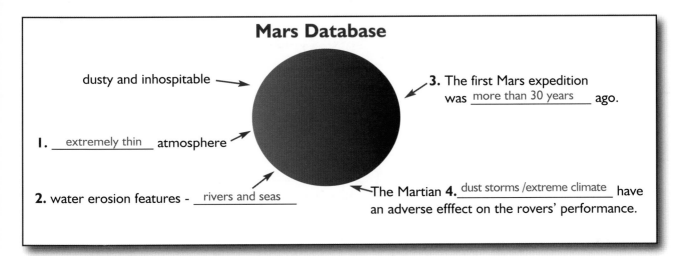

Mars Database

dusty and inhospitable →

3. The first Mars expedition
was _more than 30 years_ ago.

1. ___extremely thin___ atmosphere

2. water erosion features - _rivers and seas_

The Martian **4.** _dust storms /extreme climate_ have
an adverse efffect on the rovers' performance.

2B   Questions 5 - 10 { Track 044 }

Write **no more than THREE words and/or a number** for each answer.

Mars Expeditions – in chronological order

Mars Two and Three were sent by **5**_(the) Russians_ at the beginning of the1970s.
Mars Two crashed on impact and Mars Three **6** _failed to operate_ when it landed.

In **7**___1976___, the U.S. rovers Viking One and Two were sent to Mars.
Viking Two was particularly successful, functioning for a total of **8.**_1,281 days_.

In the 1997 launch, the Sojourner rover was transported by the **9.** _Mars Pathfinder_.
The mission was of only limited success but there were significant technological
advances in the equipment used.

The American rover, **10.** _the Opportunity_, has outlasted the others.
It was launched in 2004 and was still operational in October 2011.

Glossary

*rover: a usually uncrewed vehicle, used especially in
exploring the terrain of a planet and its satellites*

2C   Questions 11 - 14 { Track 045 }

Write **no more than THREE words and/or a number** for each answer.

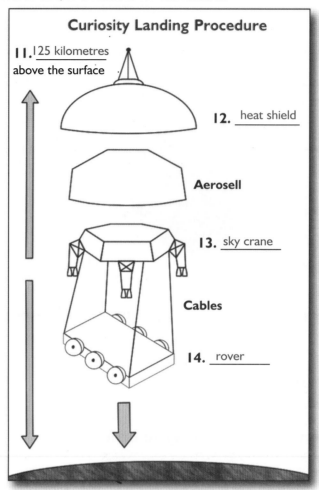

Curiosity Landing Procedure

11. 125 kilometres above the surface

12. heat shield

Aerosell

13. sky crane

Cables

14. rover

Hint:

In charts and diagrams, IELTS language is at its most technical and you may not recognise some of the vocabulary used in the labelling. Therefore, it is a good idea to think of possible ways of pronouncing the unknown word(s) before you begin listening.

Main Listening

Task 3 { Track 046 }

You will hear a guest speaker talking to students in the *Science Department* about computer-controlled cars.

3A   Questions 1 - 3

Write **no more than THREE words** for each answer.

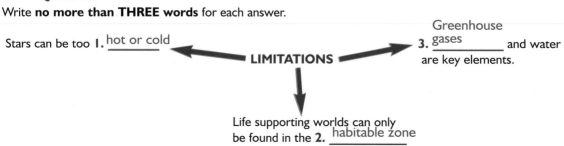

Stars can be too 1. hot or cold

LIMITATIONS

Greenhouse
3. gases _____ and water are key elements.

Life supporting worlds can only be found in the 2. habitable zone

3B   **Questions 4 - 8** { Track 047 }

Write **no more than THREE words** for each answer.

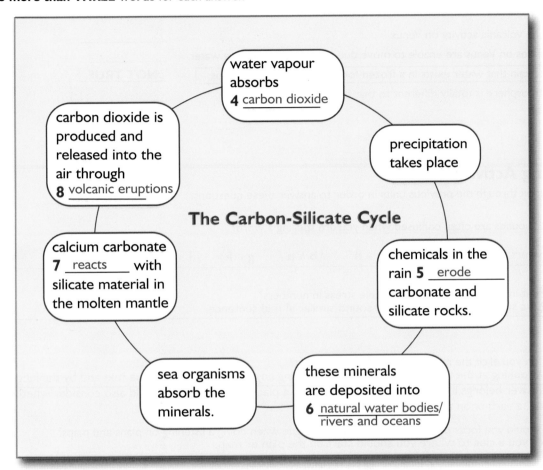

The Carbon-Silicate Cycle

water vapour absorbs **4** carbon dioxide

carbon dioxide is produced and released into the air through **8** volcanic eruptions

precipitation takes place

calcium carbonate **7** reacts with silicate material in the molten mantle

chemicals in the rain **5** erode carbonate and silicate rocks.

sea organisms absorb the minerals.

these minerals are deposited into **6** natural water bodies/ rivers and oceans

3C   **Questions 9 - 12** { Track 048 }

How Earth's atmosphere retains heat

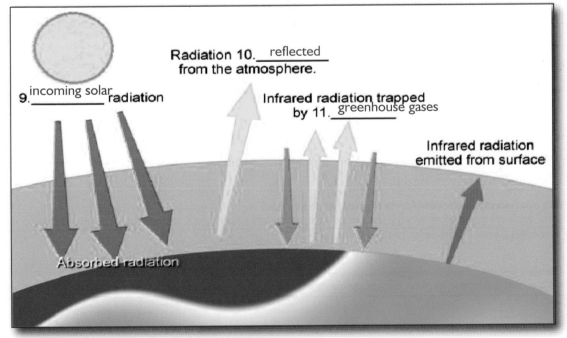

Radiation 10. reflected from the atmosphere.

9. incoming solar radiation

Infrared radiation trapped by 11. greenhouse gases

Infrared radiation emitted from surface

Absorbed radiation

12. Which one of these facts about our neighbouring planets is **NOT TRUE**?
Choose the correct letter, **A**, **B**, **C** or **D**.

a. There used to be volcanic activity on Venus. _____

b. The tectonic plates on Venus are unable to move due to the lack of surface water. _____

| **c.** Scientists are certain that water exists in a frozen form in the Martian ice caps. | **NOT TRUE** _____

d. The Martian atmosphere is totally different to that of Venus. _____

Post-listening Activity

You will need to look through the previous units in order to answer these questions.

1. Unit 1 – Which sounds are often confused when you are spelling a word?

1. Possible answers: **t & d   / s & f /   m & n   / b & p /   g & k   / l & r /   s & z**

2. Unit 2 – Why is it important to recognise syllable stress in numbers?
Because numbers such as thirteen and thirty sound similar in mid sentence.

3. Unit 3 – How do you elicit the main idea from a listening text?
This is done by looking at the title, if available, and underlining any key information in the text and by thinking about what kind of answer belongs in each space – e.g. a number, a place or a date. You should also consider whether it could be a noun, a verb or an adjective

4. Unit 4 – Why should you focus on the early part of the dialogue when doing a listening on plans and maps?
Because it gives you a clue to where you should start on the plan or map.

5. Unit 5 – What are 'content words' and why are they important?
Content words are usually nouns, verbs and adjectives and they contain the main ideas.

6. Unit 6 – What is meant by the term 'distractor'?
It means other information which may confuse you while listening.

7. Unit 7 – Why can pronouns be important when you are doing a listening test?
They often substitute key words and may be part of an answer.

8. Unit 8 – How can word form change in gap-fill exercises?
It cannot.

9. Unit 9 – What are two more complex forms of multiple choice task?
The number of answers per task may vary. You may have to match a letter to a statement. You may have to find the correct or incorrect answer from a list of possibilities.

10. Unit 10 – What kind of charts and diagrams (examples) can you find in an IELTS test?
You may find bar and pie charts or flow diagrams. You may also come across an illustration of a process, cycle or how something works.

IELTS

LISTENING

EXAM GUIDE

LISTENING PAPER: SECTION 1

What's it all about?

Listening Section One features a conversation between two people, either face-to-face or on the phone. The subject is a topic of general interest; for example, making a reservation at a restaurant or booking a course of study. There will be one or two tasks. One of the tasks is typically note completion. This section will contain an example and 10 questions.

What's it testing?

Your understanding of specific information such as dates, everyday objects, places, numbers etc. is being tested. Spelling is also being examined in this section.

What about a closer look at the tasks?

The most common task used in this section is Note Completion. This requires you to fill in the gaps in the notes someone makes during a dialogue.

The notes will always be in the same order as the information you hear.

Tables, sentences and forms will also be seen in this section – these are essentially note-completion exercises, too. You complete the table / sentence / form with the missing pieces of information.

What do I have to do?

Basically, you have to:

(1) Read over the questions on Section 1 of your paper in the time allowed.
(2) Listen to a conversation that will be heard once only.
(3) Write one/two/three words and/or a number or date in each gap in the notes. (*Note: you will be told the maximum number of words you will need to write at the beginning of the task - it will be written in the instructions*)
(4) Write the exact words you hear.
(5) Spell everything correctly.
(6) Transfer your answers to your answer sheet at the end of the listening test.

Time for a closer look at Spelling:

If you are asked to write the name of a street, place, person etc., it will be spelt out for you. You should be very familiar with the names of the letters of the alphabet as you will only hear the recording **once**.

Mini-task 1: { Track 049 }

Match the sounds of the letters (Column A) to their written form (Column B), as in the example.

Column A	Answer	Column B
Example Sound	G	H
Sound 1	H	S
Sound 2	X	X
Sound 3	S	W
Sound 4	M	G
Sound 5	W	M

Mini-task 2: { Track 050 }

Listen to some words being spelt out and write down what you hear.

1. _____ onomatopoeia _____
2. _____ evangelistic _____
3. _____ Bairnsdale _____
4. _____ infinitesimal _____
5. _____ amelioration _____
6. _____ prejudicially _____
7. _____ Inverness Caledonian Thistle _____

Time for a closer look at Numbers:

You might be asked to write down a year, a price, a phone number, the numerical part of an address etc. in the exam.

Mini-task 1:

Match the sounds of the letters (Column A) to their written form (Column B), as in the example.

Column A	Answer	Column B
Pound	**Pence**	Cents
Dollar	**Cents**	Pence
Euro	**Cents**	Cents

Remember:

- When we say a phone number, 0 can be pronounced 'oh' or 'zero'.
- When we discuss money, we can use the singular or plural form of the currency we are referring to.
  For example:
  £5.50 = Five Pound Fifty or   Five Pounds Fifty

Mini-task 2: { Track 051 }

Listen to the sentences and write the numbers that you hear below.

1. _____ £5,445 _____
2. _____ £145.50 _____
3. _____ 25p / 25 pence _____
4. _____ 3rd / third _____
5. _____ 181st _____
6. _____ $15,000.99 _____
7. _____ €8,005.05 _____
8. _____ 0845 373 548 _____
9. _____ 911 438 882 _____

Remember:

- Read the word you've written – if you can't say it, ask yourself: *'Have I missed a vowel?'*.
- When a letter is repeated, i.e. 'EE', instead of saying it twice, we say 'double'; in this case: 'double E'.

Time for a closer look at Dates and Measurements:

Dates can be written in different ways to get a mark. The following dates are all correct and would fit the instruction 'write one word and/or a number':

   (i) 3rd March   *(ii) March 3rd*   *(iii) 3 March*   *(iv) March 3*

Measurements can be written in different ways too. Twenty-five metres, for example, can be written as:

   (i) 25 metres/meters   *(ii) 25m*   *(iii) is an abbreviation; this is perfectly fine.*

Mini-task 1: { Track 052 }

Listen to the sentences and write the dates that you hear below.

1. _____ 10th July 1985 _____
2. _____ 14th February _____
3. _____ 8th March 2001 _____
4. _____ December 2014 _____

Mini-task 2: { Track 053 }

Listen to the sentences and write the measurements that you hear below.

1. _____ 10 foot 9 inches / 10' 9'' _____
2. _____ 5km (kilometers/kilometres) _____
3. _____ 800kg (kilograms) _____
4. _____ 453ml (milliliters/millilitres) _____

Remember:

- We say dates like 1945 or 2015 as *'nineteen forty-five'* and *'twenty fifteen'*.
- But for years between 2000 and 2010, we can say *'two thousand and ...'*
  - 2002: *'two thousand and two'*, for example.

Putting it all together.

Now, let's look at some exam-type questions for Listening Section One.

Listening Section 1, Task 1: { Track 054 }

Complete the notes below. Write no more than two words and/or a number for each answer.

Safari Holiday

Example	Answer
Holiday lasts	......2...... weeks

Holiday begins on 1 ...May 21st.......... .

Minimum age is 2 .....14......... years.

Each day, group covers 3 .....20km........ of the Serengeti plains.

Holiday costs 4 ...$675.99........ per person sharing.

All food included except 5 ...evening meals....... .

{ Track 055 }

More information is available at www. 6 ......safarafaria......... .com.

Price is inclusive of 7 ....flights........... .

The holiday promoter offers a 8 .....guarantee......... of your money back if all the animals on the list are not spotted.

Tour is popular, so travellers are advised to 9 ...book early............. .

A 10 .....deposit............ of £500 is required to secure your place.

Listening Section 1, Task 2: { Track 056 }

Complete the notes below. Write no more than two words for each answer.   { Track 057 }

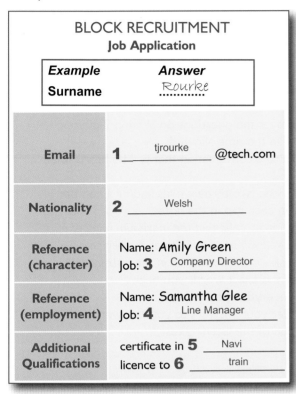

BLOCK RECRUITMENT
Job Application

Example	Answer
Surname	Rourke

Email	**1** _tjrourke_ @tech.com
Nationality	**2** Welsh
Reference (character)	Name: Amily Green Job: **3** Company Director
Reference (employment)	Name: Samantha Glee Job: **4** Line Manager
Additional Qualifications	certificate in **5** Navi licence to **6** train

Current Vacancies

Location	Name	Department	Requirements
Golder's Green	BELL LTD	Technical Support	**7** experience with Navi
Sutton Common	NOX LTD	**8** Graphic Design **9** Animation	2 years Quaddrome
10 Central London	COMP PLC	Software Development	qualified trainer

Remember:

- Always read the instructions and check how many words you can write in each gap.

- Always look at the notes and form/table headings. This will give you some idea what the recording is about.

- The information will always be in sequence on the recording. In a table, therefore, you should answer row-by-row.

- Because you only hear the information once, always keep up with the speaker. If you miss a gap, forget about it and move on (but do guess it at the end - you've nothing to lose!).

Listening Section 1, Task 3: { Track 058 }

Complete the notes below. Write no more than two words and/or a number for each answer.

BILL TO:

EXPRESS FREELANCING, 25 BEECHCROFT MEWS,
3 _Streatham_ COMMON, SW15 5TW

PURCHASE ORDER NO: 4 _528635478_

INVOICE

DATE	NUMBER
1 21 July	**2** 251

(or similar)

{ Track 059 }

QUANTITY	DESCRIPTION	UNIT PRICE	AMOUNT
2	Print **5** Cartridge	**6** £45.00	**7** £90.00
10	Glossy **8** Photo Paper	£ 50.00	£ 500.00
		V.A.T.	**9** 22.5 %
		TOTAL	**10** £722.75

LISTENING PAPER: SECTION 2

What's it all about?
Listening - Section 2 features a talk / speech / announcement / recorded message / radio excerpt given by one person. The speaker is sometimes introduced by another person. The subject is a topic of general interest; for example, what's on in the local area, a place of interest etc. There will usually be two tasks. Any type of listening task could be seen, but multiple choice, labelling, matching and flow-chart completion are particularly common. This section will not contain an example. There are ten questions.

What about a closer look at the tasks?
Okay, let's start with basics:
(1) You hear the recording only once.
(2) Before the recording is played you are given time to read the questions.
(3) Listen carefully to the introduction because it tells you what the recording is about.
(4) The questions always follow the order of the recording.
(5) Transfer your answers to your answer sheet at the end of the Listening Test.

What's it testing?
This section tests to see if you can understand specific factual information and select relevant information from what you hear.

What do I have to do?
Basically, you have to:
(1) Read over the questions on Section 2 of your paper in the time allowed.
(2) Listen to a conversation that will be heard **once** only.
(3) Write one/two/three words and/or a number or date in each gap in the notes.
(Note: you will be told the maximum number of words you will need to write at the beginning of the task - it will be written in the instructions)
(4) Write the exact words you hear.
(5) Spell everything correctly.
(6) Transfer your answers to your answer sheet at the end of the listening test.

Time for a closer look at Paraphrasing:

In many exam tasks you will be required to choose the correct answer from a list of options. The options will express the ideas and information on the recording in different words to those which are actually heard.

Mini-task 1:

Match these words / phrases (1-10) to ones with similar meanings (A-J).

	Column A	Answer			Column B
1	frequently	B	A		a ringing endorsement
2	quite forceful	D	B		on a regular basis
3	high end	I	C		haggle
4	a maximum of	F	D		pushy
5	a wide variety	H	E		organise a rendezvous
6	a gentle way	G	F		no greater than
7	conveniently located	J	G		mild-mannered
8	arrange a meeting	E	H		a large selection
9	negotiate	C	I		upmarket
10	a positive review	A	J		easily accessible

Mini-task 2: Multiple Choice { Track 060 }

Choose the correct letter, A, B or C.

1 The bakery is now situated
   - **A** beside the tavern.
   - **B** opposite the river.
   - **C** above the dry cleaners.

2 Every Tuesday and Thursday, the bakery sells
   - **A** local products.
   - **B** speciality products.
   - **C** discounted products.

3 The bakery is well-known for
   - **A** its friendly welcome.
   - **B** the quality of its products.
   - **C** offering good value.

4 What change has taken place at the bakery in the last few months?
   - **A** A franchise has acquired it.
   - **B** Production has been scaled back.
   - **C** It has been renovated.

Remember:

- Notice how the information on the recording has been paraphrased in the questions above. In Question 1, the prepositions on the recording are different to the ones written down here, for example.

- Although the questions should follow the order of the recording, it is not necessary for each set of options (A, B and C) to do so.

- Use the time alloted to read the questions wisely. For example, reading Question 2 should prompt you to think about the kind of vocabulary associated with 'local products', 'speciality products' and so on.

Mini-task 3: Multiple Choice { Track 061 }

Choose TWO correct letters from the options A-E.

1 Funding for the new community centre came from which two sources?
   - **A** the local government
   - **B** town residents
   - **C** a local company
   - **D** a multinational company
   - **E** a special state agency

2 On what grounds was a complaint lodged with the planning authority?
   - **A** the community centre would attract undesirable characters to the area
   - **B** the community centre would drive away existing businesses
   - **C** the community centre would be built on the site of a listed building
   - **D** the community centre would create a noise disturbance
   - **E** the community centre would be an eyesore

Remember:

- It is very important to read the instructions carefully before answering the questions. Here it is necessary to choose two options instead of just the one.
  In general, a 3-option MCQ will normally require you to select **one**, while a 5-option MCQ will require you to select **two** options.

Mini-task 4: Map Labelling { Track 062 }

Write the correct letter, A-H, next to questions 1-5.

1. Sports Hall ....B....
2. Gym ....C....
3. Art and Craft Centre ....A....
4. Recreation Zone ....D....
5. Theatre ....F....

Remember:

- The speaker will say exactly where you are on the map at the beginning if necessary (although in this case, you will obviously start from the entrance).

- The letters on the map are not in the same order as the places you hear mentioned, but the places written down in the question are in the right order.

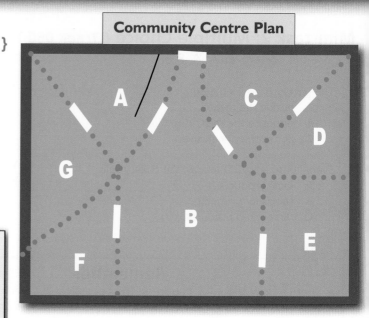

Community Centre Plan

{ Track 063 }

Mini-task 5: Diagram Labelling

Choose five answers from the box and write the correct letter, A-H, next to questions 1-5.

A	Blow Holes
B	Tubercles
C	Baleen
D	Lip grooves
E	Flukes
F	Ventral Grooves
G	Dorsal Fin
H	Pectoral Fin

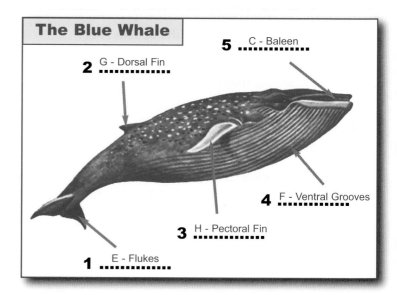

The Blue Whale

5 .... C - Baleen

2 G - Dorsal Fin ....

4 F - Ventral Grooves ....

3 H - Pectoral Fin ....

1 E - Flukes ....

Remember:

- There are always more items in the box than you need (in this case 3).

- You will hear the information you need in the same order as the numbering of the diagram.

- The words in the list may be mentioned in any order.

Mini-task 6: Matching { Track 064 }

The following are essential requirements for which roles? Write the correct letter, A, B or C, next to questions 1-5.

Essential Requirements

A own car

B third-level qualification

C flexibility

1 catering manager ....B............

2 catering assistant ....A............

3 sous chef ....B............

4 waiter ....C............

5 maitre d ....C............

Mini-task 7: Matching { Track 065 }

Which advantage is mentioned for each of the following hotels? Choose FIVE answers from the box and write the correct letter, A-H, next to questions 1-5.

1 The Great Britain ....E............

2 The Savoy ....H............

3 The Grand ....C............

4 The Wimbledon ....A............

5 The Arc ....G............

Advantages

A good location

B efficient service

C spacious rooms

D complimentary breakfast

E nice decor

F friendly staff

G wide range of facilities

H top-class restaurant

Mini-task 8: Revision

Answer the questions below about Listening Section 2.

1 How many tasks are there usually in this section? ....two............

2 How many questions are there in Section 2? ....ten............

3 Is Section 2 comprised of a monologue or a dialogue? ....monologue............

there may be a brief introduction by another person, but students answer questions based on the monologue which follows

4 How many times is the recording played? ....once............

5 What is allowed before a switch from one task type to another? ....time to read the related questions............

6 List the four task types we have looked at in this section without referring back to previous pages in the book:

(i) ....Multiple choice.... (ii) ....Diagram Labelling.... (iii) ....Map Labelling.... (iv) ....Matching....

Example 1: Section 1 Question { Track 066 }

Write NO MORE THAN THREE WORDS AND/OR A NUMBER for each answer.

Note:

The following pages contain additional practice material for Sections 1 and 2.

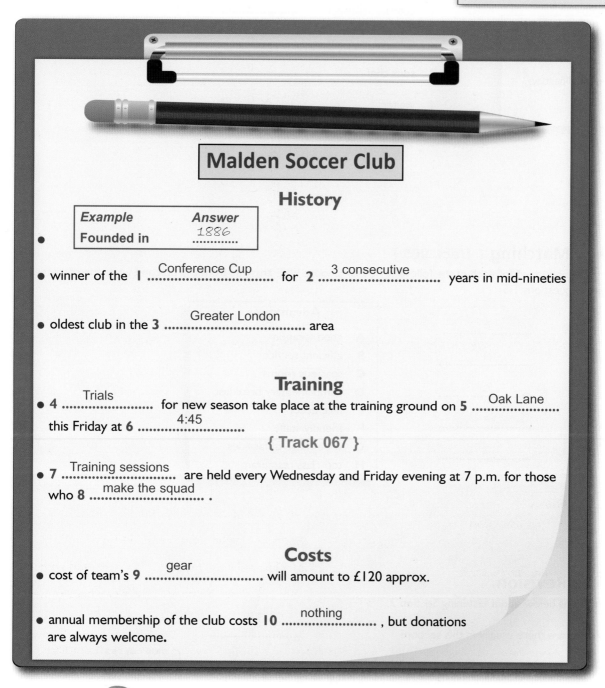

Malden Soccer Club

History

Example	Answer
Founded in	1886

- winner of the **1** Conference Cup for **2** 3 consecutive years in mid-nineties

- oldest club in the **3** Greater London area

Training

- **4** Trials for new season take place at the training ground on **5** Oak Lane this Friday at **6** 4:45

{ Track 067 }

- **7** Training sessions are held every Wednesday and Friday evening at 7 p.m. for those who **8** make the squad .

Costs

- cost of team's **9** gear will amount to £120 approx.

- annual membership of the club costs **10** nothing , but donations are always welcome.

Remember:

- The words you hear are often different from the words in the notes, except for the word(s) you have to write; try to practise paraphrasing, therefore, to help you see how information can be communicated in different ways while still retaining its meaning.

- Use the time you have before the recording starts to look at the gaps and try to predict what kinds of information you should be listening for, i.e. place names, numbers etc.

Example 2: Section 1 Question { Track 068 } { Track 069 }

Write NO MORE THAN THREE WORDS AND/OR A NUMBER for each answer.

Model / Feature	Inspirat	Chaser	Gel 2.0
Example: <u>camera</u>	1.0 MP integrated webcam	4.0 MP integrated webcam	integrated 1. <u>webcam and microphone</u>
Power	6-cell battery: 5 hours of battery life	9-cell battery: life: 8 hours 2. <u>as standard</u> .	6-cell battery: 4.5 hours of battery life
Display	14 inch	15 inch	3. <u>17.3 inch</u>
Hard Drive Memory	4. <u>500GB</u>	5. <u>750GB</u>	6. <u>250GB</u> and free 7. <u>external</u> hard drive
Extras	black leather 8. <u>laptop case</u>	Pixtra 500 9. <u>colour printer</u>	one year's 10. <u>warranty</u>

Example 3: Section 1 Question { Track 070 }

Write NO MORE THAN THREE WORDS AND/OR A NUMBER for each answer.   { Track 071 }

Example	Answer
Agent name:	<u>Andy</u> Johnson

From 22 Jun to 14 Sep in Austria:

Offering 1 <u>flights & accommodation</u> in a 4* hotel for 7 nights.

Includes 2 <u>guided tours</u> and 3 <u>rental car</u> .

4 <u>Meals</u> are extra.

Hotel boasts 5 <u>luxury spa</u> .

From 10 Aug to 25 Aug in 6 <u>(the) Netherlands</u> :

Offering a 6-night, accommodation-only holiday.

Hotel located near 7 <u>Amsterdam</u> and within

8 <u>walking distance</u> of many of the city's best-known

landmarks.

9 <u>Breakfast & dinner (or food)</u> included in the price.

10 <u>Special discount</u> for families.

Remember:

Look at numbers 1-10. They go across the table row-by-row. We know, therefore, that we will hear the information in the table in the same order: row-by-row (with row 1 coming first). If the numbers went down column-by-column, we would hear the information in column 1 first, followed by column 2 and so on.

Example 4: Section 2 Question { Track 072 }

Questions 11-14

Write the correct letter, A-F, next to questions 11-14.

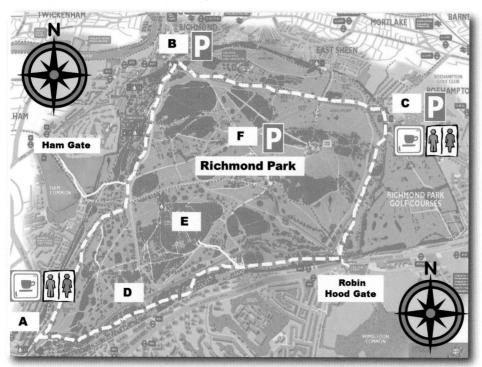

11	Kingston Gate	A
12	Car Park	D
13	Isabella Plantation	E
14	Pen Pond	F

{ Track 073 }

Questions 15-18

Choose the correct letter, A, B or C.

15 The plantation is
- **A** an area of woodland.
- **B** an area of preserved bogland.
- **C** an open area separating woods.

16 The park's name probably derives from
- **A** a staff member's relative.
- **B** a past feature of the park.
- **C** the daughter of a one-time park ranger.

17 The plantation contains
- **A** man-made water features.
- **B** natural streams and ponds.
- **C** one pond and several streams.

18 We can imply that
- **A** all plant species found there are native to the park.
- **B** a collector is responsible for planting the entire area.
- **C** some plant species have been introduced from other areas.

Questions 19 and 20

Choose the two correct letters from A, B, C, D and E.

19/20 Which plants flower in spring?
- **A** irises
- **B** lilies
- **C** rowans
- **D** magnolias
- **E** daffodils

Example 5: Section 2 Question { Track 074 }
Questions 11-15
Write the correct letter, A-H, next to questions 11-15.

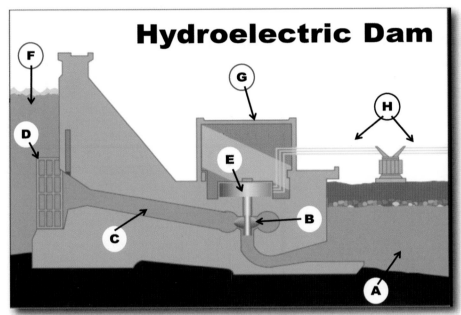

11	Intake	D
12	Penstock	C
13	Turbine	B
14	Generator	E
15	Powerhouse	G

Remember:
- There will always be more options than you need. In this case there are 8 options, A-H, and only 5 are required. It is important, therefore, to listen very carefully and look for features that differentiate items close together on the diagram in order to identify each answer correctly.

- Often, diagram and map tasks test your knowledge of language used to express where things are, so be familiar with prepositions of place, direction-giving language etc.

- Do not leave any answer blank when filling in your answer sheet. You should guess any questions that you did not get the answer to; negative marking does not apply (there is no penalty for guessing and getting an answer wrong).

{ Track 075 }

Questions 16-20

Choose five answers from the box and write the correct letter, A-H, next to questions 16-20.

16	Three Gorges Dam	F
17	Itaipu Dam	A
18	Jinsha River Complex	B
19	Churchill Falls Dam	E
20	Grand Coulee	C

A Largest annual generating capacity
B Largest dam under construction
C Largest dam construction in North America
D Largest existing dam construction
E 35 TW-hours annual production capacity
F Largest instantaneous generating capacity
G Oldest construction in the Americas
H 5,429 TW-hours annual production capacity

Remember:
- The dams are in the order you hear them, so listen for each one in turn.
- Three options are not needed.
- The options may not read exactly as they are said in the recording; some words may have been paraphrased - this is done to test your range of vocabulary.

Example 6: Section 2 Question { Track 076 }

Questions 11-14
Write NO MORE THAN THREE WORDS for each answer.

Wicklow Mountains National Park Trails

Garryknock   R756

Oakwood   Laragh West   Oldbrid Rahe Glend

Sevenchurches   R756   R115

Wicklow Mountains National Park   Glendalough   Laragh

Ballardpar

Trail Name:

11 .... Lower Mountain Road

12 .... Valley Circle Walk

13 .... Peak Path

14 .... Summit West Trail

Questions 15-20 { Track 077 }
Write the correct letter, A-G, next to questions 15-20.

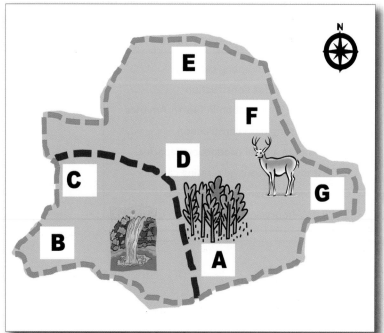

15	**Lookout Point**	F ....
16	**Roundwood Reservoir**	G ....
17	**Blessington Lakes**	C ....
18	**Hikers' Store**	A ....
19	**O'Reilly's Pub**	D ....
20	**Peak-view Lake**	E ....

Remember:
- Read the question carefully and, in the case of tasks like 11-14 above, know the word limit for your answers. This will help you focus on the key words you are looking for.

LISTENING PAPER: SECTION 3

What's it all about?
Listening Section 3 features a **discussion between two to four speakers**; i.e. between one or more students and/or a university teacher(s). The subject is **some aspect of academic life**; for example, a past or future project.

There will be **up to three tasks**, and **ten questions**. There is a brief pause in the discussion between the parts that relate to each separate task as in all sections of the Listening Test, except Section 4.

What's it testing?
Your understanding of key facts and ideas and how they relate to each other is being tested, as is your ability to identify speakers' attitudes and opinions.

What kinds of tasks might I be asked to complete?
In this section, it is not uncommon for any of the task-types to appear; that means you can expect to see up to three of: flow-chart completion, diagram labelling, map labelling, multiple choice, information matching, note completion and table filling.

What do I have to do?
Basically, you have to:
1) Read over the questions on Section 3 of your paper in the time allowed (*remember, the recording will pause between tasks and you will then be given some time to read the questions related to the next task*).
2) Listen to a conversation that will be heard once only.
3) Answer ten questions related to the recording.
4) Transfer your answers to your answer sheet at the end of the listening test.

Time for a closer look at Flow-charts:

Flow-charts require you to follow the development of a discussion. The steps in the flow-chart are in the same order as what you hear on the recording.

Mini-task 1: Flow-chart - Type 1 { Track 078 }

Complete the flow-chart.
Choose FOUR answers from the box and write the correct letter, A-G, next to questions 1-4.

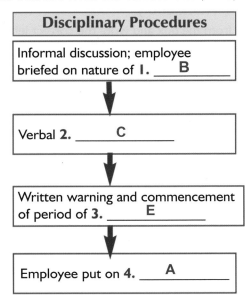

	Disciplinary Procedures
A paid leave	Informal discussion; employee briefed on nature of **1.** ___B___
B infringement	↓
C reprimand	Verbal **2.** ___C___
D dismissal	↓
E probation	Written warning and commencement of period of **3.** ___E___
F trial	↓
G agreement	Employee put on **4.** ___A___

Remember:
- Look at the list in the box and the flow-chart before you begin.
- Focus on each question in turn.
- Items A-G may be mentioned in any order.

Mini-task 2: Flow-chart - Type 2 { Track 079 }

Complete the flow-chart below. Write no more than three words and/or a number for each answer.

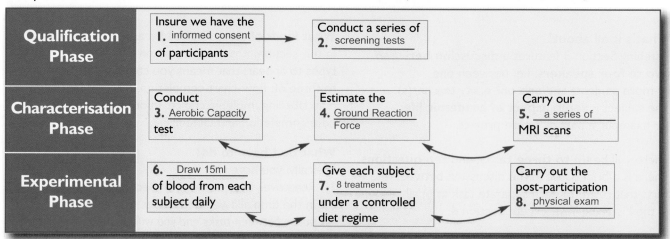

Qualification Phase	Insure we have the **1.** informed consent of participants → Conduct a series of **2.** screening tests
Characterisation Phase	Conduct **3.** Aerobic Capacity test → Estimate the **4.** Ground Reaction Force → Carry our **5.** a series of MRI scans
Experimental Phase	**6.** Draw 15ml of blood from each subject daily → Give each subject **7.** 8 treatments under a controlled diet regime → Carry out the post-participation **8.** physical exam

Remember:

- Do not exceed the word limit stated in the instructions.

- The questions will appear in the same sequence as they are heard in the recording; in this case phase-by-phase, horizontally.

- Scan the words before and after each gap. Not only will this give you some context for the subject matter, it may also give you a clue as to what to listen for; i.e. we can tell that gap 6 is probably a number (volume of blood).

- Identify cues you can use so that you can anticipate when an answer is coming. The most obvious cues here are the 3 phases; listen out for mention of each one. For gap 8, the obvious cue to listen out for is the point at which the conversation moves to discussing what happens after the experiment has been completed - 'post-participation'.

Time for a closer look at Diagram Labelling:

Diagram labelling requires you to **transfer the information you hear on the recording, to a simple picture or plan.** You will need to be able to follow the range of language which can be used to express where things are located in relation to one another. You should also be familiar with descriptive language that might be used to identify shapes, features, characteristics etc.

Mini-task 3: Diagram Labelling { Track 080 }

Label the diagram below. Choose five answers from the box and write the correct letter, A-H, next to questions 1-5.

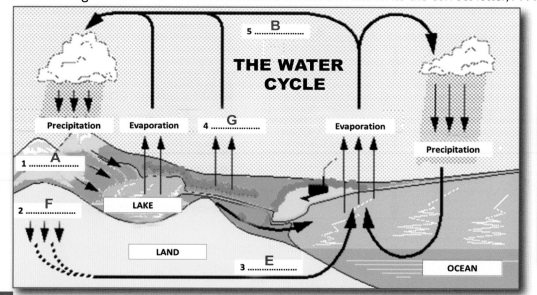

THE WATER CYCLE

A surface runoff
B vapour transport
C condensation
D underground runoff
E return flow
F percolation
G transpiration
H respiration

Mini-task 4: Diagram Labelling { Track 081 }

Label the diagram below. Choose three answers from the box and write the correct letter, A-G, next to questions 1-3.

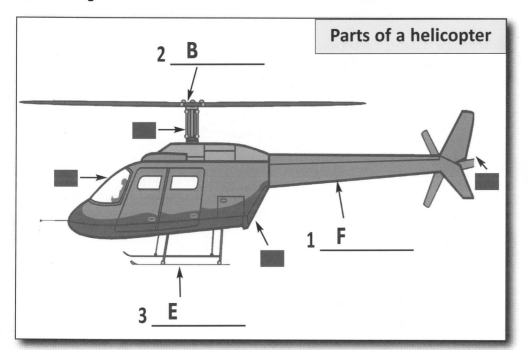

Parts of a helicopter

2 **B** _____

1 **F** _____

3 **E** _____

A drive shaft
B main rotor
C engine transmission
D tail rotor
E skids
F tail boom

Mini-task 5: Diagram Labelling { Track 082 }

Label the diagram below. Write the correct letter, A-E, next to questions 1-3.

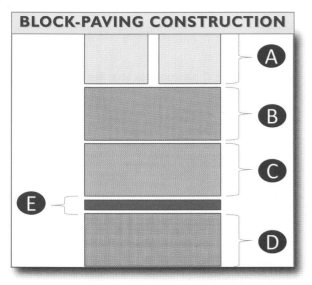

BLOCK-PAVING CONSTRUCTION

1	Damp-proof material	**E**
2	Mortar bed	**B**
3	Basecourse macadam	**C**

LISTENING PAPER: SECTION 4

What's it all about?

Listening Section 4 features a **lecture,** a **talk or** a **presentation** - in other words, there will only be one speaker, who will normally be addressing a live audience. The subject is a **topic of academic interest**; for example, a scientific or historical subject.

There will be **up to 3 tasks**, and **10 questions**.

This section is the **only section** of the **Listening** where the recording is normally played **from start to finish without any pauses** between tasks.

What's it testing?

The extent to which you can understand and distinguish between ideas (reasons, causes, effects, consequences etc.) is being tested in this section. You must be able to follow the way the ideas are organised (main ideas, specific information and the attitude of the speaker) and interpret the speaker's opinion.

Accurate spelling is essential (as it is anywhere on the test where note-completion exercises, in which you have to write down the word(s) you hear, are present).

What kinds of tasks might I be asked to complete?

In this section, it is not uncommon for any of the task-types to appear; that means you can expect to see up to three of: flow-chart completion, diagram labelling, map labelling, multiple choice, information matching, note completion and table filling. However, the emphasis is often on note-completion tasks, which appear regularly.

What do I have to do?

Basically, you have to:

(1) Read over the questions on Section 4 of your paper in the time allowed (you should read over all the questions at the beginning of the recording as you will not be given any additional time between tasks).

(2) Listen to a talk that will be heard once only.

(3) Answer ten questions related to the recording.

(4) Transfer your answers to your answer sheet at the end of the Listening Test.

On the next page, we are going to focus on **Table Completion,** a type of note-completion task that features regularly in this section.

Time for a closer look at Table Completion:

- Table completion requires you to follow a talk step-by-step, and complete a table which gives a record of the information that you hear.

- The order of the question-gaps in the table and the table layout will typically follow the order of the information heard on the recording, row-by-row or column-by-column.

- A table-completion exercise is basically a form of note completion; therefore, you must spell your answers correctly on the answer sheet and you must write the exact word(s) you hear.

- Pay close attention to the word limit for each gap as specified in the instructions and do not exceed it.

Mini-task 1: Table completion { Track 083 }

Complete the table below.
Write no more than two words for each answer.

	Habitat	Threat	Notes
The Box Jellyfish	The Philippines, Australia and other 1 .... tropical areas	Each 4 .... tentacle has enough toxicity to kill 50 people	Also known as wasp jellyfish
The Asian Cobra	The Indian 2 .... subcontinent	Potentially 5 .... lethal venom without prompt medical aid	Does not have most 6 .... toxic venom but causes most deaths
The Mosquito	The Mosquito has a 3 .... global presence	Carries disease; humans become infected once bitten	Transfers 7 .... deadly diseases .... to over 70 million people annually

Remember:

- The information in the recording will follow the same sequence as the questions; therefore, follow the table down, column-by-column.

- Look for cues to help you anticipate when the next piece of missing information will be heard; i.e. you should know to listen out for gap 6 after hearing the phrase 'wasp jellyfish' mentioned.

- You will always hear the exact word(s) you need, but its context may be worded differently from the table.

- If you miss an answer, forget it; always keep up with the recording as you only hear it once and must focus all your concentration on each gap as the key word(s) are being spoken.

Mini-task 2: Table completion { Track 084 }

Complete the table below. Write no more than three words for each answer.

Name	Origin	Features	Notes
Australian Warm blood	Developed in Australia from a breeding program involving Austrian 1 ...cavalry horses...	Hardy, disciplined animals	Bred for dressage and 2 ...show jumping......
Thoroughbred	Developed in England when native mares were crossbred with 3 ...oriental stallions...	Hot-blooded horse famous for its agility 4 ...and speed......	Excels as a racehorse 5 ...on the flat...... and over jumps
Irish Sport Horse	Developed from the crossbreeding of Irish Draught and Thoroughbreds	Known for its natural athletic ability and fantastic jumping talent	Excels in the show jumping arena and in 6 ...eventing......

Remember:

The information in the recording will follow the same sequence as the questions; therefore, in this case, focus on each row in turn.

Example 1: Section 3 Question   { Track 085 }

Questions 21-24.
Choose the correct letter, A, B or C.

21 According to the students' research
   A house prices are very high.
   B house prices are falling.
   C house prices have stabilised.

22 The students regard it as a letters' market
   A as rent is low.
   B as demand for rental property over the next year will push rents up.
   C as now is a good time to buy a property.

23 The students plan to buy
   A the right to manage a property for a fixed period.
   B a property in full.
   C a share of a property.

24 If the students buy a property, they anticipate having
   A monthly expenditure of £700.
   B monthly income of £700.
   C a profit of between £1,000 and £1,200 per month.

Questions 25-29. { Track 086 }

Complete the flow-chart below.
Choose SIX answers from the box and write the correct letter, A-I, next to questions 25-29..

Steps in the Leasing Process

Apply for a mortgage; present bank statements, proof of income and evidence of no **25** ....A.......... .

↓

Set a budget and calculate the estimated total cost of investment, inclusive of fees, **26** ....I........ .

↓

Choose a location and research the area considering important factors like commute times, **27** ....H......... and the rate of crime.

↓

Explore the market for possible **28** ......G.......... and register with local estate agents.

↓

Arrange some viewings and place an offer on the property you are most satisfied with.

↓

Complete the deal, settle all process-related fees and pay **29** ....D...... .

Advantages

A outstanding debts

B rates and charges

C criminal record

D stamp duty

E buyers

F rental income

G investment opportunities

H transport connections

I deposit and repayments

Question 30. { Track 087 }

Choose the TWO correct letters from A, B, C, D and E.

30 The students' proposal has been rejected on the grounds that

A a hypothetical investment of £100,000 is very high.

B the business plan was poorly written and structured.

C their business idea had little scope for expansion

D they did not demonstrate their business skills.

E a grant of £100,000 is not available.

Example 2: Section 3 Question { Track 088 }

Questions 21-24
Complete the flow-chart below.
Choose FOUR answers from the box and write the correct letter, A-G, next to questions 21-24.

Process of Gathering & Collating Data

Carried out a **21** ....G....... of the selected area, dividing it into residential, commercial and industrial zones.

↓

Sourced old maps and information on past planning initiatives from the **22** ......A........... .

↓

Placed the **23** ......D..... into different categories to make it more manageable. Each 25-year **24** .....F... was designated a separate category.

Advantages

A library

B results

C study

D data

E time

F period

G survey

Questions 25-28 { Track 089 }
Of which period, A, B or C, are statements 25-28 true?
Write the correct letter, A, B or C, next to questions 25-28.

25 Agricultural land was highly prized. ...A......

26 The choice was made to focus a lot more resources than ever before on infrastructural schemes. ...C......

27 The city skyline began to change dramatically. ...C......

28 Heavy industry was much more evident than light industry. ...B......

Period

A 100 - 76 years ago

B 75 - 51 years ago

C 50 - 26 years ago

Questions 29-30 { Track 090 }
Choose the correct letter, A, B or C.

29 We can imply that
   A city planners look more kindly on business than residential applications.
   B skyscrapers used as office space have earned a bad reputation.
   C all build proposals must meet much more difficult criteria for approval now.

30 Heavy industry refers to
   A commerce and I.T. firms.
   B the tertiary sector.
   C large factories and production facilities.

Example 3: Section 3 Question { Track 091 }
Questions 21-29

Whose views are represented in the statements below?
Write the correct letter, A, B or C, next to questions 21-29.

A	Ralph
B	Max
C	Janet

21   Very sceptical about writing a group critique.
A
....

22   Dislikes both the concept for the movie and the way it was produced.
A
....

23   Feels a deliberate attempt to tap into a broader viewership backfired.
B
....

24   Questions the casting decisions made by the director.
B
....

25 / 26 Critical of the length of the movie.
B ....   C ....

27   Suggests a more informed opinion is got by reading the novel.
A
....

28 / 29 Was touched by how the story concluded.
B ....   C ....

Question 30 { Track 092 }
Choose the correct letter, A, B or C.

30   Max does not like Ralph's accusatory tone; what is Ralph accusing him of?

    A   not being very good at researching things

    B   taking the course too seriously

    Ⓒ   not having a genuine interest in the course

Example 4: Section 4 Question { Track 093 }

Questions 31-40

Complete the notes below. Write NO MORE THAN THREE WORDS for each answer.

25th July: Notes from lecture 23

✍ It is not enough to build up a large portfolio of properties for sale; you must also be prepared to spend some of your time assisting buyers, who may need help determining their budget, or who may have concerns about the house-buying process.

✍ First-time buyers usually have a limited amount of cash not tied up and struggle to raise their 31 _____deposit_____ .

✍ These buyers offer better long-term revenue-generation potential provided you can get their repeat business. If you want to deal with first-time buyers, you should be ready to advise them on all the financial aspects of house-buying, in particular 32 _____how to raise_____ funds, which is often the hardest part of the process.

✍ There are often mechanisms in place to provide low-income buyers with 33 _____financial support_____ ; be aware of these.

✍ To qualify for financial assistance under the government-supported HomeBuy scheme, cumulative 34 _____household income_____ should not exceed £60,000 per annum.

✍ Besides the government's first-time buyer schemes, many 35 _____private initiatives_____ also exist.

✍ If you qualify for the HomeBuy scheme, you are responsible for 70% of the 36 _____purchase price_____ of your new home.

✍ 30% of the funding will come from a government 37 _____loan_____ .

✍ No 38 _____interest_____ has to be paid to the government for the first five years of the arrangement.

✍ In Shared Ownership schemes, buyers purchase a share in the home and pay 39 _____rent_____ in addition, but at a much lower rate than normal.

✍ 'Staircasing' describes a step-by-step approach through which you can buy back 40 _____shares_____ in your home.

Example 5: Section 4 Question { Track 094 }

Questions 31-33

Complete the table below. Write ONE WORD for each answer.

Tool	Use
Spot Healing Brush	removing 31 ....wrinkles.......... from areas of the neck and forehead
Clone Stamp Tool	removing blemishes around the 32 ....eye(s)........ and at the edges of the profile
Patch Tool	working on areas where the changes in shading are very 33 ....subtle..........

Questions 34-40

Complete the flow-chart below.

Write **NO MORE THAN THREE WORDS** for each answer.

Step 1 ➡
- examine the face area
- create a new layer
- change the view to full-screen 34 ....mode.........
- examine problem areas in close -up
- select the Spot Healing brush
- choose 'sample all layers' and then remove all 35 ....spots and moles....
- gradually stay away from edge details

Step 2 ➡
- tackle edge details
- select Cloning tool
- choose 'current and below' in 36 ...Tool Options...
- source copy area from an appropriate adjacent position
- click over blemish

Step 3 ➡
- next, focus on neck section
- create a new layer
- use the Spot Healing brush
- 37 ....click away.... neck lines gradually
- ensure that the selected 38 brush thickness is larger than the line itself
- switch to Clone Stamp tool for edge areas
- set the tool to Lighten Mode; 50% opacity
- work over the area at least twice

Step 4 ➡
- create new adjustment layer and select 'merge visible'
- new layer encompasses all existing edits
- select Patch Tool
- select cheek lines and move pointer inside selection
- then drag to area of clear skin and 39 ....repeat.... for each remaining line

Step 5
- now focus on areas to outside of both eyes
- usually a lot of 40 ....wrinkles.... in these areas
- to remove, create new layer and start to touch up using Spot Healing brush
- switch to Clone tool for areas close to the eyes themselves

Example 6: Section 4 Question { Track 095 }

Questions 31-40

Complete the table below.

Write NO MORE THAN THREE WORDS for each answer.

Name	Role	Strengths	Weaknesses
Eamon De Valera	• due to imprisonment, limited role in the 31 ...armed struggle... • more of a 32 ...symbolic... figure in the war • raised awareness of the Irish cause abroad	• shrewd and clever 33 ...politician... • very committed to the 34 ...cause... he was fighting for	• displayed an unwillingness to compromise • very stubborn
Michael Collins	• leader of the rebel war effort • used 35 ...unconventional... methods of engagement • launched successful guerrilla campaign	• an impressive leader militarily • a character full of 36 ...passion and charm...	• inexperienced in the field of politics and diplomacy
Lloyd George	• Head of British administration	• cunning politician and diplomat • his age only served to motivate him to achieve further successes	• coming to the end of his 37 ...political career... • his advanced age meant his 38 ...influence... was on the wane
Lord Birkenhead	• Key member of British government and negotiating team	• excellent speaker • a uniting 39 ...force... rather than one of discord • Developed a good 40 ...working relationship... with Irish delegation	• came from a very hardline position

IELTS
Listening

1 complete
Practice Test

SECTION 1   *Questions 1 - 10*   { Track 096 }

Questions 1 - 6   { Track 097 }

Complete the form below. Write NO MORE THAN THREE WORDS AND/OR A NUMBER for each answer.

RESULTS		Recruitment Agency

Let us do what we do best: finding you a JOB!

EMPLOYEE RECORD

Example	*Answer*
Surname	*Thompson*

Email	1 **jannthompson** @haught.net
Employer Reference	Name: Jane Foot Job: 2 **Head of English** at Bermuda Girls' School
Character Reference	Name: Monica Carmody Relationship: 3 **best friend(s)** since 1991
Main Occupation:	4 **English Teacher**
Additional qualifications	Diploma in 5 **special needs**
Can also teach:	6 **History** to GCSE level.

Questions 7 - 10 { Track 098 }

*Complete the form below. Write **NO MORE THAN THREE WORDS** for each answer.*

RESULTS		Recruitment Agency

Let us do what we do best: finding you a JOB!

VACANCIES

Temporary Teaching Positions			
Location	**Name**	**Duration**	**Notes**
city centre	La Salle	6-month contract	with a view to making position 7 **permanent**
near Chelsea	Chelsea Free School	8 **one year (contract)**	teacher absent on 9 **maternity leave**
10 **rural Cambridgeshire**	Cambridge	6 weeks	teacher absent on extended sick leave

SECTION 2　　　*Questions 11 - 20*　{ Track 099 }

Questions 11 - 15

Label the map below.

*Write the correct letter, **A – H**, next to questions **11 – 15**.*

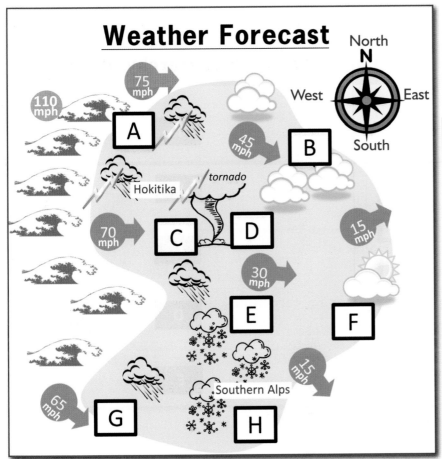

Weather Forecast

11. Christchurch　**F**

12. Collingwood　**A**

13. Bluff　**H**

14. Lewis　**D**

15. Kaikoura　**B**

Questions 16 - 20 { Track 100 }

*Choose the correct letter, **A**, **B** or **C**.*

16 From what time onwards will all roads out of Christchurch be closed?

   (**A**) 7:30 a.m.

   B 8:00 a.m.

   C 1:00 p.m.

17 What should passengers who have pre-arranged accommodation in Christchurch do when they disembark from their flight?

   A go to the customer service desk

   B evacuate to the shelters

   (**C**) go directly to their hotel

18 There will be a period of calm weather

   A until 7 p.m.

   (**B**) between 4:00 and 4:30 p.m.

   C after 9 p.m.

19 What are people travelling by car being advised to do?

   A wait until 9 p.m. before using the roads

   B drive only before 9 p.m.

   (**C**) avoid travel if at all possible

20 Coastal towns on the storm-facing side of the island have been affected by

   A strong tornadoes.

   B flash flooding.

   (**C**) power cuts.

Listening

SECTION 3 *Questions 21 - 30* { Track 101 }

Questions 21 - 24

*Label the diagram below. Write the correct letter, **A – E**, next to questions **21 – 24**.*

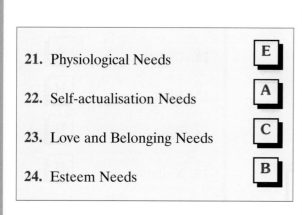

21. Physiological Needs **E**

22. Self-actualisation Needs **A**

23. Love and Belonging Needs **C**

24. Esteem Needs **B**

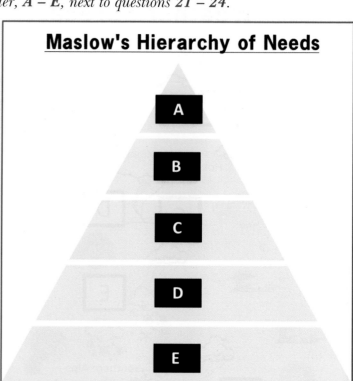

Questions 25 - 30 { Track 102 }

What need-level in Maslow's Hierarchy is the person in each case study at?
*Write the correct letter, **A, B, C, D** or **E** next to questions **25-30**.*
You do not have to use all the letters. And you may use any letter more than once.

A. Physiological	25. Case 1 **E**
B. Safety	26. Case 2 **B**
C. Love and Belonging	27. Case 3 **A**
D. Esteem	28. Case 4 **E**
E. Self-actualisation	29. Case 5 **A**
	30. Case 6 **C**

SECTION 4 *Questions 31 - 40* { Track 103 }

Questions 31 - 36
Label the diagram below. Write **NO MORE THAN THREE WORDS** *for each answer.*

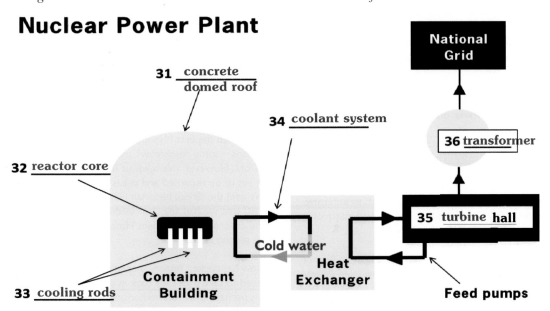

Nuclear Power Plant

National Grid

31 concrete domed roof

34 coolant system

36 transformer

32 reactor core

35 turbine hall

Cold water

Heat Exchanger

Containment Building

33 cooling rods

Feed pumps

Questions 37 - 40 { Track 104 }
Complete the flow-chart below. Write **NO MORE THAN THREE WORDS** *for each answer.*

The Fukushima Disaster: Sequence of Events

Earthquake strikes.

↓

Reactors **37** ....**automatically shut down**.. (new source of power now needed for coolant system).

↓

Diesel generators powered on.

↓

Tsunami hits after 50 minutes, **38** ....**breaching**............ sea-wall defences.

↓

Turbine halls become flooded.

↓

39 ....**Generators**............ are disabled.

↓

Back-up battery power in Reactor 1 partially fails.

↓

Core temperature and pressure inside containment building rise.

↓

Explosion next day leaves containment building's roof collapsed; meltdown is **40** ....**confirmed**...... .

UNIT EIGHT *(from page 38)*

TASK 4

You will hear a lecturer giving an introductory talk to students for their Ancient History course module.

4A
First you have some time to look at questions 1-7.
Now listen carefully and answer questions 1-7.

Lecturer: So, welcome to your introductory history lecture. Today we will be examining history in its most general terms and attempting to personalise it with questions such as what does it mean to me and how has it shaped the world that we live in. Naturally, one lecture is hardly sufficient to cover such an extensive area but I hope to provide you with enough background information to inspire you to do more research for yourselves.

I'm first going to focus on the more personal aspect of what history means to us. In the auditorium today many of us come from diverse cultural backgrounds – Europe, Asia, Australia and so on. We all have our individual cultures, don't we? Where do they come from? Why am I the way I am? This is where History comes in. Think on this; if you had been born in another country, how would your attitude to the world differ?

Take family life, for example; in European and North American culture you can see that families form tight nuclear units. Basically, the parents or parent lives with their children, without any other relatives, including the grandparents. When they come of age, the children often leave home and set up their own lives, eventually buying their own homes. All of this would indicate a prolonged period of affluence in society, which subsequently leads to greater financial independence and personal freedom at a younger age. Some may perceive this as being a positive phenomenon and rightly so - it can be. However, on the flip side of the coin, it can also form the basis for social disintegration with families drifting apart.

However, even in the most affluent societies, during times of recession this trend changes and children often stay with their parents for much longer. This is also true for people who live in economically unstable countries such as those in South America or Africa. It has been observed on countless occasions that financial constraints bring both the family and the community together creating stronger social cohesion. An example of this in Britain was during the Second World War when money was short and food was rationed. People's homes were often bombed and many lost their livelihoods but they worked together to repair their lives; women farmed the land when the men were away fighting. This is what is commonly known as community spirit, which comes to light in times of hardship – the slums of Mumbai are one of the best examples of this. Many people are often crowded into one dwelling, food is scarce, disease is rife and there is poor sanitation. Yet, despite all these obstacles, the people seem to be happy with their lives - something, unfortunately, which does not always apply to western society.

These models, however, can only serve as generalisations as there are other factors which may come in to play. For instance, they cannot be applied to family life in the oil-rich Middle East where religious laws play a key part in the social pattern. In this case, religious doctrine not financial dependence has shaped family life and society as it has done for many centuries. The importance of the extended family is paramount in these countries – with the elders deciding familial, social and political norms.

So we've covered some but by no means all the factors that affect us personally. These and others will be analysed in greater detail later on in the course.

4B
Now you have some time to look at questions 8-14.
Now listen carefully and answer questions 8-14.

So far we've summed up some of the more evident reasons for our cultural diversity and you will almost certainly find a good few more as we work through the booklist. Now, let's turn to a more panoramic approach to history. Our modern world is almost totally a product of what we have accomplished over the last seven thousand years – when the first Mesopotamian cities were established by the Sumerians – some researchers may go even further back to our first ancestors. However, this takes us back into prehistory when facts were yet to be recorded and this is not covered in our course. It wasn't until the Greek historian Herodotus emerged in the 5th century BC that we had any clear evidence to work from. His findings will be covered in the Ancient History module which will commence in the second term.

So, how has ancient history shaped the world we live in? First of all, we need to take a journey back in time to focus on the topography. This is perhaps the most immediately obvious way that our world has changed. Thousands of years ago, Europe and North America were covered with huge swathes of forest and human settlements were limited to isolated tribal communities who were often nomadic or lived in small villages. Wild animals such as bears and wolves roamed freely and man hunted for food. It is not surprising, therefore, that during this period man had to fight for survival which meant mortality was high.

However, over the centuries as the population expanded, the woodland was steadily cut down only to be replaced by ever-growing (in both size and number) human settlements. The result of this can be seen today in the form of megacities such as Tokyo and Chongqing, both with a population of around 30 million; and there are a number of cities such as Shanghai, Mexico City and New York all boasting a population of over 15 million. And according to projections these figures could rise dramatically.

Mexico City, for example, was shown to have a population of 17.1 million in the year 2000. However, by 2015 the forecast shows that it will have risen to 18.2 million. That's an increase of over a million in a matter of 15 years. Cities such as Rio de Janeiro and Beijing follow the same pattern within the same timeframe with a small but significant increase of 1-2 million. There are others, however, such as Jakarta and Lagos which appear to show an enormous increase – the figure for the latter one, Lagos, jumping from 13.4 million to a staggering 23.2 million; almost doubling the size of the population.

So, we have progressed over the course of four or five thousand years from a handful of scattered tribes living off the land to a highly technologically advanced global society with a population of over 7 billion and still growing; and with it the impending and serious repercussions of environmental destruction and mass starvation. How and why did it happen? What will happen in the future? Of course, it's not our job to predict – we're historians. But, needless to say, every fact which comes into being is history in the making and that's what makes our subject so fascinating.

Now, let's move on to the development of political systems and their influence on our lives today.